Living in Sin

LIVING IN SIN

Making Marriage Work between I Do and Death

JASON MICHELI

Fortress Press

Minneapolis

To Mike and Laura Paige
Do as I say and not as I do

CONTENTS

DECLARATION OF INTENT

The impeded stream is the one that sings.

—Wendell Berry

NUPTIAL HERMENEUTICS

In my line of work, Bible stories make convenient shorthand, so I tell people I feel like Lazarus. He's the stiff that Jesus, having wept, rescues from the grave, stinking and four days dead. Like Lazarus, I've received a reprieve from death. It's temporary. In the beginning, my cancer couldn't be staged like most other cancers, and I'll never be in remission. The doctors spare me the lie. The odds are not ever in my favor. Of course, the odds on most marriages are only fifty-fifty, so you tell me which the worse bet is.

I have something lethal latent in my marrow called Mantle Cell Lymphoma, which leaves my marriage to bear a peculiar burden. Both of us cope with the looming possibility of my death just as we also cope with our failures to live up to the "miracle" my reprieve from death has handed us. We've not yet crashed into that final clause in our wedding vows ("until we are parted by death") but escaping death, if for a time, has made "I do" more difficult.

When I awoke from emergency surgery a couple of years ago to a doctor explaining how I had a rare cancer percolating in my marrow, I thought it was curtains on the time God had given us, my wife Ali and me. Like a carpenter sizing up a difficult cut, the oncologist had stroked his beard and squinted when he delivered the news to me, packaging it all together in a single four-syllable word: incurable. Then, I thought it was closing time. Now, I know my time is just short. My death is no more likely than yours, but it's probably nearer.

Making the most of the time you've got left isn't as easy as it sounds. In fact, it's not easy at all because the *you* you bring to your new lease on life is still the old you. You're still the you who took everything—God, life, health, family, and marriage—for granted. Lazarus, the Gospel of John notes, comes back to life carrying the stench of death all over him. The Lazarus who crawls out of the tomb is unmistakably the Lazarus who was laid in the grave. Not dying is not automatically the same as a new life. After a year of stage-serious chemo, I learned the inevitable wasn't yet. And I felt bowled over with gratitude.

So I made a bucket list:

#3: Spend more time with my friends.

#7: Take my job less seriously.

#2: Be less of an asshat to my wife.

It turns out bucket lists are like New Year's resolutions. What's true about us when it comes to yoga and CrossFit is true about us in relationships too. The only consistent thing about us is our inconsistency. As soon as maintenance chemo and CT scans became my new normal, the old normal returned, albeit rearranged to accommodate my cancer. Without my even noticing it, I was back to sermon-writing on Saturdays, rain-checking drinks with friends, and insisting to Ali "Yes, honey, I'm listening."

I wasn't listening.

Dodging death may not come as a disappointment, but it can reveal the many ways you are a disappointment. Being handed a new lease on life, I assumed my marriage would automatically become new, too. You know what they say about the trouble with assumptions. I was an ass for supposing our miracle marriage would be easier than any other marriage. Don't get me wrong. I'm not saying our marriage before cancer or since cancer wasn't or isn't good and happy and loving. It was and it is (as of this writing). But it's also difficult and aggravating and heartbreaking and, more often than I'd ever choose, humiliating.

I was a dumbass for assuming the crucible of cancer would make the crucible called marriage any less of a challenge. A pastor should know better—the chemo-poison may keep the cancer in my marrow at bay, but there is no cure we can conjure on our own for what Scripture says ails us. Bucket list in hand, I entered our *new* marriage as naively as so many of the couples I've wed with vows and rings.

No matter how much I tell brides and grooms I don't want to preach on 1 Corinthians 13 ("Love is patient. Love is kind . . ."), nine times out of ten I lose. When it comes to kissing the bride, I've learned that it's a good idea to remind every groom that just because they can kiss like that on *The Bachelor*, it doesn't mean they should do so in the sanctuary. I've learned that George Strait's country song "You Look So Good in Love" is a tacky song for the bride's processional, and that it's even worse when the CD skips and the usher shouts from the back of the banquet room: "Should we start over or should I just press pause now?" And I've learned that when the bride or groom asks if their twelve-year-old cousin/nephew/niece/brother/sister can sing a pop song in the wedding to say no, and say no again and again if necessary because never again will I stand up front with a fake smile plastered on my face, wishing I was plastered, as a twelve-year-old boy, whose voice is newly in the throes of puberty, tries to make Bill Withers's "Ain't No Sunshine" sound worshipful.

When it comes to weddings, I've learned the hard way, especially when it comes to couples who want to write their own wedding vows.

At one of the weddings I performed right after coming off a

year's medical leave for the stage-serious cancer I still carry in my marrow, the couple asked me if they could write their own vows. As vogue as it is for cast members of *Friends* to do so, most folks don't request to write their own vows. This was the first time, and having no prior negative experience, I said sure. Unsuspecting, I didn't ask to see their vows prior to the wedding rehearsal. The rehearsal was on a crisp October afternoon, on a farm surrounded by mountains on fire with fall colors. I walked them through the first half of the service.

When it came time for them to exchange vows, the bride and groom turned to face each other, pulled out folded-up pieces of notebook paper, and proudly read what they'd written.

Let's just say they weren't English majors.

What they'd come up with sounded vaguely like Donald Trump pitching the script for *Jerry McGuire*: I think you're beautiful. The best! I can't take my eyes off you.

The groom said: "I've never felt this way before. You knocked me off my feet for undressing you with my eyes." (Yes, he really said that). The bride said, "Your carefree abandon makes me smile and laugh." The bride apparently didn't realize her declarations sounded as profound as a pair of panties that read "Juicy."

They read their "vows" and then looked at me for approval.

"What do you think?" the bride asked me, beaming.

"Um, well, it's certainly *something*," I replied. "But . . . everything you've come up with . . . it's about how you feel right now, at this point in your lives."

"Exactly," the groom said. He too was beaming.

Since cancer, I'm quicker to cut past the bullshitting and get to the point. So I said, "I hate to break it to you, but you're not always going to feel the way you do right now."

The groom asked me what that was supposed to mean.

"She's not always going to be this beautiful. And you, you're going to gain weight, and by the looks of things, in five years you're not going to have any hair."

"And you," I turned to the bride, "you might love his carefree abandon now but wait until you've got bills to pay and children to clean up after. Give it time and the hands you can't keep off him now will instead be reaching out to strangle him."

It was right about then that I looked past the bride and groom and saw the bride's mother blanching. She was covering her mouth, like she'd just thrown up a little bit, horrified, wondering what insane person had just body-snatched the pastor.

Now I'll admit it, I'm a sinner as much as the next bastard, and maybe fourteen hours before their wedding wasn't the best time to squash their romantic notions.

"You should stick with the time-tested traditional wedding liturgy," I said to them. "You'll thank me for it later."

"Really? Is that right?" the groom pushed back, his soon-to-be balding temples were pulsing and red with anger.

I nodded.

"If the old-fashioned service is so special, then you tell me, *Preacher*, why in the hell it's all about Jesus. Dude never got married and all he did was hang around with twelve single guys. Sounds pretty queer to me."

I'd like to say he meant queer as in *odd* or *irrelevant* to the nuptials at hand, but judging from the fact that the groomsmen were all wearing Dickies brand work vests with their boutonnières, I think probably not.

Still, his question was not irrelevant, and I don't know that before my brush with death I would've noticed or appreciated his point about how odd it is that, for Christians at least, marriage begins with a liturgy framed around an unmarried man, for whom love and crucifixion are synonymous.

The closest to marriage Jesus ever got was forgiving an adulteress on the one hand and showing up late to a wedding party on the other. In Cana, Jesus turned a whole lot of water into a whole lot of vintage-tasting booze, a handy skill to have when you're running with a dozen thirsty bachelors. What the bridal magazines and the marzipan couples on top of cakes obscure, the marriage liturgy makes unavoidable: the marriage service is only incidentally about the prospective mister and missus. Wedding planners always try to relax the wedding party by comforting them with the lie that all eyes will be on the bride; meanwhile, the wedding service would have all our eyes on neither the bride nor the groom but on the cross above them on the altar wall. The liturgy directs us away from ourselves and to the God revealed to us in a single, suffering Christ who was crucified for our sin.

Bride and groom do more with vows and rings than cement their love story; they celebrate the love story Christians call the gospel. With vows and rings, they give themselves over to be transformed by the perceptions of one another, transformed, that is, from awful, goddamned sinners into graced occasions of joy. The vows they make to one another, the exclusive love they pledge to give one another, their commitment to go forward with each other even though the way is not certain (will never be certain), their promise of love to one another reminds us of how God Loves each of us, a capital-L love that saves all of our lives by losing our lives in God's own death. In the same way the lovers of a Van Morrison tune become a parable for the bride and groom as they dance their first dance on the parquet floor, the vows and rings bride and groom exchange make them a parable of how the Beloved makes us God's beloved by loving sinners to the grave and back.

Bride and groom, by their nuptials in the church, perform a parable of how God loves us all in Jesus Christ; therefore, it stands to reason that what husband and wife do in marriage is no less a parable of what the church says and believes about God's love revealed to us in Jesus Christ.

The reason nine out of ten couples come back to me insisting that they want 1 Corinthians 13 for their wedding service is that for a canon with sixty-six books in it, there just isn't all that much about marriage in the Bible, and the stories of married folk we do find in the Bible aren't exactly the kind you can read aloud in front of flower girls. For example, Father Abraham not only tried to cut his son Isaac's throat but passed his wife off as his sister, pimping her out to Pharaoh. His grandson, Jacob, meanwhile "got to know" the wrong girl by, ahem, mistake. His son, Judah, made the same mistake with his own daughter-in-law, Tamar, who cheated him by disguising herself as a prostitute, which says a lot about her. Ruth meanwhile, whose "entreat me not" testimony gets read and sung at many weddings, took her future in her own hands by giving a rich man, Boaz, a hummer on the floor of the threshing room. Boaz's grandma was Rahab, a "working girl" who betrayed her own people. Everyone knows about Boaz's great-grandson, David, the Donald Trump of his day. David was a power-hungry, narcissistic Peeping Tom and predator.

Those are just some of the names in Jesus's family tree.

The marriages in the Bible make *Game of Thrones* look like a *School House Rock* segment. Outside of a few antiquated household codes ("wives submit to your husbands," the single Paul suggested to the church council in Ephesus, I'm guessing to no avail), the Bible doesn't contain a lot of happy, healthy marriages in it. Nor does the Bible offer much in the way of hands-on marriage advice. Instead what Scripture gives us, without so much as an embarrassed flushed face, is messed up marriages populated by sinners whose lives seem engulfed by fires of their own making. Scripture would have us, in other words, go to it looking not for advice on how to improve and perfect our marriages but for the incarnate and perfect love of God in *these* marriages and relationships.

The marriages in Scripture are not models to emulate; they are messages to apprehend the grace of God incarnate in Jesus Christ.

Likewise, our own marriages, whether they're on fire with love or sin (likely both at once) are parables of the prodigal Father who loves sinners without fine print or conditions. Nothing convinces you that you do not deserve God's extravagant grace like escaping, for a time at least, the wages of sin. Nothing reminds you that you have not given your lover the life you vowed like living when you expected to die.

Having come through stage-serious chemo and living now with incurable cancer, my eyes are as fresh as a newly hewn grave to the extent to which I deserve neither the woman to whom I'm married nor the grace of God in whose name we were wed seventeen years ago in a university chapel. With the clock running down, you become aware that every moment is a gift you don't deserve, which, in church parlance, makes my time with Ali grace and makes me a sinner. Like a man whose sudden blindness tunes his ears sharper, cancer has heightened my awareness to how I am no better, and in some ways maybe worse, than all those other married guys in the Bible. And, though I think she's perfect, Ali too is probably only perfect in that she's a sinner perfect for a sinner like me. Our marriage, then, imperfect though it may be, is like all those others in the pages of Scripture, a parable of One who is more perfect than either us.

The wedding liturgy always begins with what the prayer book calls the "Declaration of Intent." It's the caveat emptor of the service, making sure the bride and groom understand what they're about to get themselves into for perpetuity. Perhaps a similar caveat is in order here: what I offer you in this book is not exactly a *Christian* book *about* marriage. Such books are a dime a dozen, and, given the preponderance of messed-up marriages in Scripture and the dearth of practical marital advice in the Bible, I tend to think the counsel of such books is, more often than not, malarkey.

What I intend instead is a marriage book about Christianity; that is, a kind of *nuptial hermeneutics*. I want to offer you a diorama of our marriage and, through it, show you how to speak Christian. People are forever wondering if Christian faith has

any real-world application. To my mind, there is no better labo-
ratory to test, by hard and harrowing trial-and-error, the coher-
ence of Christian speech than the person you'll watch floss for
the rest of your life, or some fraction thereof. If the wedding
liturgy makes every couple in love a parable of God's love, then
I want to use the parable of my own life and love with Ali to
explore what the hell Christians, Protestants in particular, mean
by words like *sin* and *grace, forgiveness* and *crucifixion*. If it's true
that Jesus Christ reveals the grain of the universe, then learning
what these words mean in the context of a marriage just might
be what saves it.

It's saved my "miracle marriage."

Her body is a wonderland, as John Mayer puts it in his corny
song, but her body is also the means by which I better understand
what it means to belong to another body: Christ's own. Baptism
into that body is not, like marriage, something you choose; it's
something you live into. But both, baptism and marriage, are
vocations that give you a life you could not have chosen nor fore-
seen. By reflecting on my life with my beloved, I hope to help you
live into your life with the Beloved.

Full disclosure: I don't know any secrets about relationships.

Having worked with hundreds of couples on their own relationships, I've come to the conclusion that there are no secrets
to relationships. Such secrets would only tempt us to bypass the
hard but life-giving work that Christians call dying to self. So be
warned. I don't know any secrets. I only know my need, and I
know that, whether you realize it or not, your need is the same as
mine.

In every aspect of our lives but especially in our marriages,
we need more than advice. Like Lazarus, we need either a good
undertaker or we need someone who can raise the dead; that is,
in between the folly of our "I dos" and the death that tears us
asunder, we need grace to make marriage work.

TRANSLATOR'S NOTE: WHEREIN I JUSTIFY THE POTTY LANGUAGE YOU'LL ENCOUNTER ALONG THE WAY

Do-ce-tism: [dō-se-tizm], n., The heretical belief that Jesus was not really human but only appeared to be human; therefore his suffering, fear, joy, and foul-mouth were only apparent not actual.

The incarnation is one of the primary theological convictions of the Christian faith.

We believe the Holy Spirit *overshadowed* Mary and, through her, God took flesh in Jesus of Nazareth. That's our claim at Christmas. As St. Athanasius put it, God became what we are so that we might become god.

God became what we are, in all our dirty, unpleasant particularity. Jesus was fully human, as the Nicene Creed says. Not *mostly* human. Not *pretty much* human with all the crappy, embarrassing, or difficult parts left out.

Most often Christians use words like *incarnation* or "God taking flesh" without getting down to specifics about what that entailed or included. It's like when it comes to the incarnation, there's a subconscious part of us that screams: "Stop: TMI!"

Like it or not, in Jesus, God had a body just like yours.

Jesus may have been without sin, but he wasn't without boogers. Jesus not only wept, you can bet your keister that he wiped his ass. There aren't any carols about it, but part of what Christians profess at Christmas is that Mary's boy (a.k.a.: The

Lord of Hosts) grew up to spit, piss, poop, and fart. He had moles on his skin, dirt underneath his fingernails, and he had a smell that I'm sure his mom could recognize on his clothes. He dreamed dirty dreams and had wet ones too. Contrary to pop legend, I don't think Jesus had a thing with Mary Magdalene, but since he was fully human, you can be sure she gave him, at least once, a something that rhymed with *loner*.

That Docetism was outed in the first years of the faith shows how from the ancient church onward, Christians have been discomfited by the implications of their own claims regarding the incarnation. Since then as well Christians have proven themselves to be functional Docetists in that they reflexively expect Christ's vicars, people like me, only to *seem* human.

By my reckoning, I've performed somewhere between 150 and 200 weddings, and nearly every wedding reception I get seated at the (goddamned) Grandma Table. The only people the newly minted Mr. and Mrs. know who can speak passable Christian without blushing usually were born in Hooverville hovels. Also, they assume people like me, with collars and faith, don't talk like real people. Pastors, they think, don't harbor the same fears and frustrations as you, the same fault lines don't run through our relationships like they do yours, nor do we ever express them in the same fully human, four-lettered language as you.

They're certainly not to blame for supposing this. Come Sunday morning, you can go to Fill-in-the-Blank Church in Anywhere, USA, to find a robed reverend like me who appears to be human only by accident, betraying none of the actual anxieties that afflict you, the Monday-Saturday crowd. The church in the West is not in decline because it's desperate for more vanilla pastors.

I talk as I talk because there's no dearth of collared types who avoid talking as you talk. If it's pastel niceties and cross-stitched Scripture-speak you're looking for, then I'd suggest you either tune in to Joel Osteen next Sunday morning or you can take my seat next to Grandma. We have plenty of Grandma Tables in church. They're called pews. If that's your bag, go with it.

But if you're given to blushing or bemoaning ("A pastor shouldn't talk this way!"), then whatever you do, don't turn the page.

In what follows, I've tried to make myself as vulnerable as my wife will allow. I've written about my naked self. I've even written about myself without any clothes on. And I've attempted to speak about it in the same way you speak, in ways that are both sacred and profane. I use the language I do to make a point that is tonal as much as it is theological. While Christians adorn our sanctuaries with stained glass and retreat from the world, this does not mean Christians imagine the world (or life, for that matter) is so fragilely constructed. I've tried to give it to you unvarnished, without the protective sheen of stained-glass language, so that I may appear to you to be as fully human as the one I believe was fully God.

And, also, because writing about the most vulnerable part of my life scares me shitless.

CHAPTER 1.

HUMP DAY

Sex is like pizza. Even when it is bad it is good.

— Mel Brooks

The Oughts always accuse.

—Martin Luther

SITTING SHIVA IN THE BACKSEAT OF A CHEVY

I hadn't thought about it in years: my mom climbing into the trunk of my father's maroon Bronco II and laying down silent and rigid, covering herself with a worn, woolen emergency blanket. It was midwinter, exhaust-stained snow plowed up along the edges of our Ohio driveway.

Sometime later my father got into the driver's seat and switched on the ignition. Lighting another Vantage cigarette and pushing the heat lever to the far right of the panel, he pressed play on the tape deck and waited for the truck's engine to warm. He then pulled out of the long gravel driveway, unaware that he was betraying his nightly routine to a suspicious stowaway. He drove through the slush of the neighborhood and into town, crossing the Y-Bridge and parking outside a Kozy Korner or some similar bar.

Lighting another cigarette, he hopped out of the truck and entered the bar. After waiting what she judged to be a safe amount of time, my mother pulled off her woolen veil and climbed over the rear seat to ease her way out of the car. She walked up to the bar's neon window adorned with Christmas lights and peered in. Already steeled by expectation, she spied my father at the bar with a woman. Buttoning her coat, she walked the four miles home. I was nine or ten.

My mother didn't confront my father that night. I don't think. Only much later did my mom confess it to me. If she conveyed it out of any sense of absolution, I couldn't tell.

My father was an alcoholic and unfaithful in that order. Who knows if the former alone was responsible for the latter.

As a celebrant of weddings and a counselor to marriages, I know how seldom we consider the memories that make us and, later, shape the marriages we make. Usually we wait until death nears to take stock of our life and those lives that made it so. We wait, I suspect, because we lack the nerve to see ourselves as we truly are, the self only God and our spouse see.

I was diagnosed with a rare, incurable cancer a couple of years ago. I thought I was going to die. Then I learned I wasn't going to die (yet). *Miracle* is the word that people laid on me. It feels as heavy as Superman's cape.

Handed a reprieve from the grave, I suddenly felt my life needed to merit the miracle I'd been given. I began to think my marriage needed to merit this miracle too. You don't need to read any further to know that no spouse should have to shoulder such a burden of expectations.

And no marriage can.

I joke that whenever I stop moving, people start to throw dirt on me. Only Ali laughs at that joke, and, even then, I suspect it's not because she thinks it's funny. "Don't encourage him," she's constantly telling anyone who will listen. It's a mercy on her part. She knows I need to hear it, her laugh. Like Lazarus, I know more keenly than most that my reprieve is a not a resurrection.

The house always wins and, odds are, sooner not later someone else wearing a black robe and a white stole will intone over me the inexorable math I've proffered at some five hundred gravesides: from dust I came and to dust I will return.

To circumvent death, which we all do our best to do, is ultimately not possible. But to have terminal cancer is to know it now as your constant companion.

Having come through the crucible of stage-serious chemo, I now live with incurable cancer by keeping the grim reaper at bay on a monthly basis. "Maintenance chemo," my oncologist scrawls in awkward block letters on the xeroxed calendar he hands me prior to my next infusion. He always pats me on the knee and then shakes my hand before handing it to me.

When my fortysomething friends use the word *maintenance*, they're most likely referring to hiring a personal-fitness trainer or trimming their pubes. My doctor's stoic pat on the knee, however, leaves no room for illusions that what I'm maintaining isn't the level of chemo-poison in my blood or the level of MCL in my marrow, but me—my life.

Every time, the countdown on my chemo pump feels to me like it's counting down more than the last drops of the poison that paradoxically keeps me alive. The clear bag of meds always scrunches up, like a juice box, as it empties into me—a damn good simile considering how my nurse usually has as much trouble getting the needle into me as a kid in soccer cleats does getting the straw into a Capri Sun. Living with what I've got, I've come to feel for that juice box. There comes a point when you're just tired of being stuck all over all of the time.

At one such infusion, I nodded my head at the scrunched up bag of Rituximab and joked to my wife, who was sitting beside me and encouraging my nurse's ribbing: "It looks like we're trying to wring every last moment we can out of our wedding vows."

Wait for it.

". . . It's probably not worth the medical bills."

Ali looked up from the game of solitaire on her iPhone and

cocked her eyebrow and pursed her lips in her fake angry face, and with the same tone of voice with which she'd reply "Yes, I'd like cash back, thank you" she says, "Screw you."

She flinched first, smiling. The freckled lines on the sides of her dark-brown eyes are always her tell. And then we both of us laughed—the kind of laughter that's a mess of grief, joy, terror, and something like craving, pregnant hunger. The kind of laughter I hear at funerals where jokes are like chicken soup offered to salty tears—mourners, hoarse from sobbing, gorge on ham biscuits and half-a-dozen deviled eggs only to belly laugh bits of it out their mouths while tender-aged grievers sit Shiva by getting out of their ill-fitting dress clothes and getting it on in the backseat of their Chevy in the church parking lot. We laughed that sad and frightened and hungry but ready-to-hump kind of laughter because we are trying to wring every last damn minute from our marriage.

"Earth to earth, ashes to ashes" arouses all kinds of emotions. It's grim news that's just as likely to make you horny and hungry as it is to leave you feeling harried or hopeless. I mourn losing the luxury of knowing it only secondhand, the guy in the collar watching the hurting without a care in the world of his own.

I've parsed the wedding vows out to brides and grooms, phrase by phrase, so many times now that I've got them memorized. But truth be told, I didn't give them a thought when I promised them to Ali. God, how glibly I echoed the lines the officiant fed me: "forsaking all others until we are parted by death." What was I thinking? I hadn't even been to a funeral. In the moment of our nuptials, I'd only been aware of Ali's dad's doofy tears, the crack of honest vulnerability in both our voices, and how much I ached to get out of my sweat-soaked suit and into bed with her.

I hadn't yet considered the weight of sin and death, certainly not enough to notice how passive the wedding vows make death's appearance in a marriage sound. "Until we are parted by death" makes the Grim Reaper sound like Alfred, Bruce Wayne's butler: a welcome and polite gentleman who ushers an accommodating husband and wife to their respective seats in a theater not made with hands.

But like the Dread Pirate Roberts in *The Princess Bride*, I'm not dead yet, and, more than the meds, it's true love that keeps me alive. I know that sounds like cloying sentimental bullshit. What I mean is, the latter (love) keeps me enduring the former (chemo).

Like Lazarus, I've been apprised of death's dimensions. I've got the stench of it all over me as surely as I've got the metallic twinge of nausea in the back of my jaw. I now know personally what I'd already learned professionally: death visits no married couple as kindly as the wedding liturgy implies. Death is always more like a home invader against whom every spouse is well within their rights to stand their ground. I prefer the language the apostle Paul uses in the Bible to that of the prayer book: death is an enemy, the Last Enemy, Paul says, like one who's been in love. Death is a foe God is determined to destroy.

"Forsaking all others until the Enemy defeats one of us, leaving the other beloved vanquished and lonely and stuck in time to cling to their yellowed 4×6 photos and fading memories." That's what the vows should say. They should brace us for what's to come. No niceties. Or they should at least be as honest as your average love song. Even the most fraught relationships are held together by a complicated love that makes death the most violent of intruders. Even unhappiness can become an intense elixir we can't live without. When it comes to passion, you either can't live with her or you can't live without her. Either makes an empty euphemism like "parted by death" as much a lie as "kick cancer's ass."

As a workaday pastor with a Sunday sermon always hanging over his head, I thought I knew what a deadline felt like, but then I came down with Mantle Cell Lymphoma, and the life I assumed would one day flash before my glaucoma-stricken eyes feels instead condensed into averages and expectations from the

MD Anderson Clinic, like a speculative line item in some actuarial ledger.

With lethal, incurable cancer in my marrow, I tell people that I can feel my blood coursing through me like sand in an hourglass. I felt proud of that way of putting it. But then, after some sediment in my memory chipped free, I realized I'd actually just stolen it from the opening lines of the soap opera my mustachioed grandmother watched when I was a kid: "Like sand through an hour glass so are the days of our lives." It's an appropriate bit of plagiarism, I suppose, given how my monthly appointments with mortality double as calendar invites to self-pity and melodrama. The only difference is that most actors find themselves in soap operas at the beginning of their careers. The chemo ward has the feel of a lot of things, but beginnings aren't one of them.

See, even that last line is sufficiently melodramatic for a soap opera. It's also true.

I suspect that's why over the course of stage-serious chemo and several dozen maintenance infusions, I've never once seen a soap opera playing on any of the TVs in the ward.

HUMP DAY

Today, the second day of Lent, *Ballykissangel* is playing on the television on the wall. I've been here so often, an average of four days per week for a year and then two days a month thereafter, that my phone recognizes the Cancer Specialists Wi-Fi signal. The woman next to me, on the other side of the drywall partition with the plum-purple glasses and weathered gray hair, is sobbing. Her gasps sound like drowning. My phone doesn't recognize that, but I do.

Her cancer, I can tell from the fresh, pink chest port wound, is a recent discovery. Maybe hers was found like mine, a lump in the shaving mirror. Maybe she, too, thought it was nothing, nothing at all.

Earlier, in the waiting room, she'd been cracking Murphy's law–type jokes and genuflecting to the power of the positive thinking. I'm not surprised she's the one sobbing now. The beats of my infusion pump ring like a metronome tracking the time of her mournful music. Anything less than an overwritten sentence like that preceding one just doesn't capture the unforced melodrama of this place. All of us here, we've all been conscripted into a *Days of Our Lives* episode.

I came here yesterday, too, for the checkup and lab work necessary to green light the fresh chemo-poison.

Yesterday was Ash Wednesday.

I could tell from the knock on the door (too soft and abrupt) that it wasn't Dr. D. That's how often I've been here.

Dr. D was away, she said, before launching into: "So, have any signs of your symptoms returned yet?"

Yet?! She rubbed her hands together to warm them, and then she searched for tumors along the back of my neck.

"Should we be expecting them to return?" Ali asked. "Already?" She was, I could tell, trying not to cry.

"Well, what your husband has is very aggressive. When it comes back, you'll definitely know it."

I could tell from the look in Ali's eyes that the voice in her head was running: *When?!* Holy shit, lady! At least your hands are warm because your bedside manner sure isn't.

Dr. D had told us during my last checkup that he didn't plan to order any of the post-treatment follow-up scans typical of other cancer protocols.

"Why not?" Ali had asked.

"When, if, it comes back—frankly, we'll find it in his blood first, or we'll find it on him. The thing about Mantle Cell," he said, "is we won't really know anything about how he's responded until about twenty-four months after your last treatment."

"But, that's like Thanksgiving after next," Ali said.

He nodded, pastorally it seemed to me. "Let's hope Thanksgiving with your in-laws is the worst of the holiday."

He smiled when he saw me chuckle. I don't know if he saw that Ali didn't. She didn't chuckle at all.

"For most people, it's the uncertainty they struggle with, but you seem to be different, handling it better, in stride. I imagine that could be because of what you do, but I'm going to guess it's really because of who you are."

"Don't let me fool you. I'm still scared out of my mind."

Ditto, Ali said without words. I reached out to hold her hand.

I didn't mention to him how that week I'd be burying a man—an old one—who died of what I have. If that's not a coincidence, then Jesus has a constipating, twisted sense of humor.

The doctor who was not Dr. D laid me down on the table and felt my groin for "indications of recurrence."

She told me I could sit up, and then she flipped over a baby-blue box of latex gloves and, with a black Sharpie, illustrated the standard deviation of years until relapse for my particular flavor of incurable cancer.

Ash Wednesday isn't typically a day given over to shits and giggles, but it didn't feel very funny staring at the bell curve of the time I've likely got left.

Until.

"You didn't sign up for this. I'm sorry, honey," I told her, pushing the button for the elevator outside the oncologist's office.

"Yes, I did. Or if it makes it easier for you, I do sign up for this. I do." And she squeezed my hand like we do after we've held hands to say grace at the dinner table.

As a pastor, I've done a few vow recommittals over the years. I'm actually surprised more people don't do them. I like them a hundred times more than performing weddings. They have a simple, tender elegance to them. No ridiculous flowers or annoying photographer humping the floor to wiggle his way to the exact spot I told him I didn't want him during the ceremony.

And I like recommittal ceremonies for the wrinkles and warts the couple bring with them to the moment, all of which somehow seem to breathe new life into the ancient vows. Here's what I've learned from both recommittal ceremonies and simply watching couples' marriages change, grow, and sometimes deteriorate. Marriage requires you to say "I do" not just to the person standing in front of you on your wedding day. Marriage requires you to say "I do" to whomever and whatever that person will become, something unknown on your wedding day. It's not knowing who your spouse will become one day that makes the act of marrying another a leap of faith.

Or, to put it less religiously, it's what makes marriage a grave and foolish risk.

You don't know who your spouse is going to be twenty years hence. All you can know is that they won't be the same exact person. Marriage requires spouses to recommit—either informally or liturgically but always intentionally—at key junctures along the way of their lives together. Your spouse won't be the same person at forty-five they were at twenty-five. They won't be at sixty-five who they were at forty-five. You might discover they're terrifically insecure. You might learn they don't really like children or that they actually hate rom-coms.

You might find out they have an incurable cancer.

I've seen too many couples throw in the towel because their spouse has changed, yet they never took the intentional steps of determining how they can best love their spouse as they are now. I've seen even more people's marriages wither on the vine because they assumed what got their marriage to the ten year mark will get them another ten years. They never develop new habits, new skills, new goals, new ways of relating and emoting for the place they find themselves now in their marriage. And the marriage atrophies until the couples are no longer truly married so much as they're cohabitating. You'd never plant a seed in the ground, water it a little, and then walk away assuming the rest will take care of itself. But I see people all the time treat their marriage that way. And I know I'm guilty too.

Marriage requires you to say "I do" and then "I do" again a few more times along the way.

Leaving my oncologist's office yesterday, I drove to a nearby hospital to visit a parishioner of mine named Jonathon. He's a bit younger than me, with a boy a bit younger than my youngest. He got cancer a bit before I did. He'd thought he was in the clear, and now he's dying. The palliative-care doctor was speaking with him when I stepped through the sliding-glass ICU door. After the doctor left, our first bits of conversation were interrupted by a social worker bringing with her dissonant grin a workbook, a fill-in-the-blank sort, that he could complete so that one day his boy will know who his dad was.

I sat next to the bed. I know from both my training as a pastor and my experience as a patient, my job was neither to fix his feelings of forsakenness nor to protect God from them. My job, I knew, wasn't to do anything for him but simply to be with him.

I listened. I touched and embraced him. I met his eyes and accepted the tears in my own. Mostly, I sat and kept the silence as though we both were prostrate before the cross. I was as present to him as I could be given that all I could think about was me in that bed soon enough.

And Ali beside it.

We were interrupted again when the hospital chaplain knocked softly and entered. He was dressed like an old-school undertaker and was, he said without explanation or invitation, offering ashes. Because it was the easiest response, we both nodded our heads to receive the gritty, ashen shadow of a cross.

What the church does with oil and ash can send the wrong signal to onlookers. The point of the ashy cross Christians smear across their foreheads is that it's a *cross*. The cross marks us out not as pious people but as the opposite. The cross is a reminder the very best of our piety put God to death; therefore, on Ash

Wednesday Christians come out of the closet. With a soot scarlet letter, we freely admit that, no matter what we pretend all the other days of the year, we don't have our shit together.

I know *sin* is a dirty word in our post-Christian culture. As someone routinely thrust into the position of having to defend all Christians everywhere, I understand how other Christians have made *sin* another shameful, shaming s-word. If *sin* gets your sphincter in a twist, striking you as an impossibly antiquated word, trade it out in your mind for what writer Francis Spufford calls the HPtFTU: the "Human Propensity to Fuck Things Up."

We suck.

Every married person knows it to be true. Every married person knows they suck because every married person knows the person to whom they're married knows just how much they suck. In marrying another, we meet, maybe for the first time, the worst version of ourselves.

Sin names the symptoms of the sickness called the self we'd rather not see. There is no better venue for the stranger you call you to be revealed than marriage. To confess yourself a sinner is to admit you're afflicted with the HPtFTU. It's original to us, teaches the church in her catechism. I mean, Adam and Eve couldn't make it through a lunar cycle before they screwed up the good thing they had going *in paradise.* Maybe they would've lasted a little longer in Eden had they been single. Nowhere are we confronted daily with our propensity to screw the pooch than in our life with the person to whom we've pledged that life unto death.

Soon after saying "I do" to us, our spouse learns what only God has heretofore known about us. We're not the selves we filter through a social-media sheen. We are instead the worst text messages that we send. We are what we silently scream in the shower. We are the grudges that we hold and the arguments we relitigate in our heads. The ashen cross brands me not as someone who thinks he's holier than thou but as someone who screws up on a reliable basis.

Christians mix up their metaphors on Ash Wednesday, dust . . . ash . . . dirt . . . sin . . . death, as though the brokenness we experience in our lives and wreak in others' lives are but signs of a deeper crack in God's good creation, a fissure we fill only a fistful at a time standing tiptoe over a tomb.

Clerics call what we do on Ash Wednesday "imposing ashes." I think the rudeness implied, if often unnoticed, by the term *imposition* gets the gesture exactly right, especially when done to those in palliative care. I didn't bother to mention it to the man looming in Jonathon's ICU room with oily black dish and inky manila prayer cards, but what Christians acknowledge with ashes is as rude as death, for while the *words* we say on Ash Wednesday invite you to remember that you're going to die, the *cross* Christians smear on Ash Wednesday invites you to remember that you will do so as one neck deep in your HPtFTU. That is, you will die a beggar, asking for grace and mercy. The odds on that are holding steady at damn near 100 percent.

Living with incurable cancer can feel like it's Ash Wednesday every day. When you fear you're going to die and don't (yet), you don't just make a bucket list, you obsess over your rap sheet. You rehearse your regrets and you revisit your resentments as compulsively as a tongue that trolls over the hole where a tooth used to be.

With my own death drawn on the back of a box of latex gloves and Jonathon's own death imminent, we leaned our foreheads into the chaplain's bony thumb.

"Remember," he whispered (as though we could forget), "to dust you came and to dust you shall return."

As if every blip and beep in the ICU itself wasn't already screaming the truth: none of us is getting out of life alive.

The anthropology of Ash Wednesday, the self-assessment it imposes upon us, is rudely, brutally low, forcing us to be frank that our virtue by itself cannot bring off what it knows perfectly well how to do. When I said as much to Ali later that night after our church's evening Ash Wednesday service, both of us with soot on our foreheads, she replied with a tone of teasing indictment: "Maybe acknowledging the worst about yourself is the way to accept the worst in another."

I smiled, kissed her beside her smiling eye, and parried: "So, being able to say 'I fucked up' is the necessary precondition to saying 'I love you?'"

"It is for you, mister," she said as she began to put the dirty dishes in the dishwasher.

SAVING PRIVATE RYAN'S MARRIAGE

Jonathon's marriage both began and broke in the intensity of his illness. Like I said, the grim side of the gospel can make us horny and hopeless in no predictable way.

To get a reprieve from the grave, like Lazarus, is to wonder if between my wife and Jonathon's wife, his ex didn't choose the more prudent path. Ali doesn't deserve the sadness that, odds are, will yet come her way, and avoiding that sadness thus far has impressed upon me just how much I do not deserve Ali.

A quiet, smiling fellow, Jonathon always kept his thoughts close to the vest. I don't know if his ex left him because she thought he was going to die. I know that's the most likely explanation. I also know now, having gotten a temporary reprieve from the grave, that it's possible she left him because she feared that he would live. Maybe she feared that he would survive, and thereafter they would live not happily ever after but saddled with living up to that mushroom cloud of a word, *miracle*.

Not long after I came back to work from a year's medical leave, a parishioner sent me a text message about a twelve-year-old boy, Joshua, at my son's elementary school dying (actively so) of brain cancer. The boy's parents asked for me to sit with them. I hate my job sometimes and, just as often on those occasions, I doubt the existence of the One from whom my vocation supposedly comes. If there were such a thing as a believer's thesaurus, then *pediatric oncology* would be a synonym for atheism.

Josh's bed was decorated with sheets of printer paper scrawled in different colors with Sharpie-written Jesus speak:

"Thy will done."

"In my Father's House are many rooms"

"Let the little children come . . ."

The faith papers were arranged around him like flowers in a casket. Josh had written them before the brain tumor palsied his hands. His mother told me he lost his ability to speak that Wednesday. On Saturday he lost control of his eyes. By Sunday when I arrived his breathing was shallow and labored.

After I helped Josh's mom wash him, for several hours I held her hand, and I listened as she whispered to him, in between sobs, "It'll be okay. God doesn't make mistakes."

"God doesn't make mistakes," she kept whispering to him. But maybe I've made a mistake for believing in him, I thought.

I came back the next night. I stood by his bed and I wiped the spittle from his mouth and I rubbed his head as praise songs played on the tablet lying next to his shoulder. It was close, I could tell. So I prayed something about how Jesus says children are first in the kingdom, prayed it to the God with whom, in that moment, I was righteously pissed off. Your heart would have to be tone deaf to hear a mother's spleen-deep sobs and not feel furious at God—or feel foolish for believing in the first place.

When I left, his godmother was rubbing his feet and shouting at him, through stubborn tears, to wake up. He died just a little while later. His funeral a few days after that was the latest in a dozen I've performed where the casket is shorter than the "Must Be Taller Than" yardsticks on a rollercoaster line.

Having gotten a reprieve from the grave, I eschew the miracle talk people eagerly impose upon me. I do so because such a miracle requires a moral calculus that I cannot countenance; it's a formula that subtracts kids like Joshua before he was old enough to have his first crush only to leave me as a remainder.

I'm also allergic to the miracle-speak for less altruistic reasons: namely, it puts a huge burden on me (and my marriage) to merit that miracle. I mean, people expect miraculous survivors of rare, incurable cancer to go on eat-pray-love spiritual pilgrimages, not make blowjob jokes into the Taco Bell drive through mic with your friend Ryan while you order several boxes of Doritos Locos tacos.

Since getting my reprieve from the grave, I've thought often of that scene in *Saving Private Ryan* where the Tom Hanks character, who's already lost his entire company and is now about to lose his own life, tells the Matt Damon character, whom they've all come to rescue from certain death: "Earn this. Earn this."

It wasn't until I learned I was going to live (for a time at least) that I understood why the old and wrinkled Matt Damon character has tears in his eyes at the end of that movie. Earn this (miracle) is a godawful impossibility to impose on someone. He's probably crying because he's petrified he has not earned anything close to the purchase price of his pardon, or because after a lifetime he still has no idea how to measure if he's met the conditions of his rescue.

Spielberg could've made a sequel: *Saving Private Ryan's Marriage*. No spouse deserves to be drafted into meeting the demands hiding behind a word like *miracle*, a word that sounds like gospel, good news, but is actually it's opposite. You can bet your ash that Lazarus and Miracle Max knew it. The dead don't bear the burden the nearly dead do: to make their miracle worth it, to merit the second lease on life that Raymond Carver called "gravy."

LIVING IN SIN

Reprieves are different than resurrections.

Resurrection means that this world that God made matters, this life—our hopes, our longings, our pain, our work, our choices, our relationships, our emotions, our bodies—so matters God plucks it back from the grave. Easter means it all matters. Every kiss. Every movie and every meal, whether candlelit or in front of the TV. It all matters. Every joke, funny or not. Every moment spent with Ali and every effort spent at getting lucky with her. All of it matters. Every bit of it. All of me and every bit of my life with her.

If resurrection from the grave means every part of the life you lived matters, then a reprieve from the grave can feel like every part of your life now *should* matter. What resurrection celebrates looking back in hindsight, reprieve converts to forward-looking aspiration.

Or, worse, expectation.

In premarital counseling with couples, I routinely find myself talking anxious brides down from the dread and panic they feel. They often fear their wedding day won't measure up to the glossy, five-figure expectations handed down to them from Pinterest and bridal magazines. I don't think I truly empathized with the brides-to-be, however, until I got handed a *miracle* and felt, firsthand, the crushing weight of expectations. The cancer in my marrow not only means our marriage suffers the burden of impending doom, it means also Ali suffers the burden I often impose upon our marriage that every moment now be memorable. Needless to say, this expectation of mattering makes our marriage more significant than is healthy or wise, but it also can make every sin and slight between us in our marriage seem more significant too, a problem of scale that can turn even an Easter into an Ash Wednesday.

Put Paul's way: a reprieve from the grave can take what is gospel about the resurrection (every moment of your life *is already* significant) and turn it into an accusing command you can't possibly keep (every moment of your life *should be* significant). All those thou shalt and shalt nots in Scripture—Paul says they're inscribed not just in stone tablets but onto every human heart. So even if you don't believe in God or follow Jesus or read the Bible, the commandments manifest themselves in all the shoulds and musts and oughts you hear constantly in the back of your mind, all those expectations and demands and obligations you feel bearing down on you.

To think every moment of my marriage to Ali *should* matter only underscored how many moments didn't seem to matter at all, or mattered in the wrong way: the little white lies that closed off a conversation I was too tired to carry on, the half-listened to phone calls and the screened ones, the wasted hours drinking beer and watching crap like *3000 Miles to Graceland* or *Michael Bolton's Big, Sexy Valentine's Day Special* when I could've been getting randy with her.

To tell Ali that every moment *ought* to matter was to blame her for how our marriage fell short. We ought to argue less. We ought to make love more. You ought to laugh at my jokes more. We ought to get past what's in the past.

The oughts always accuse us.

Every marriage feels the sting of the oughts' accusation. There's the ought that tells you that you and your partner ought to pretend your life is like the picture that comes with the frame—perfect, unabated bliss, and if you're not happy all the time, there must be something wrong with the two of you. The oughts' accusation is why we crop out all the imperfection in the pictures we project out onto the world, filtering out all the unhappiness and garden-variety dysfunction. No spouse, for example, ever posts a picture of their antidepressants on Instagram, but I could field a baseball team just from the spouses in my own congregation who I know are on them. Every marriage feels the demands of the oughts, but a relationship that's gotten a reprieve from the grave bears a particular burden of expectation.

Your marriage must feel like a miracle now, every other church person says to Ali at least every other Sunday. *You two ought to be so happy all the time now that your prayers have been answered and you have more time together*, a teacher at my son's school told me in the parking lot.

"You must be flying through the Kamasutra. It must be like make-up sex all the time. Your knob must be good and polished. You two have to be on a different plane altogether now, right?!" my friend Ryan speculated between bites of popcorn during the trailers before *Creed* (which, sigh, turned out to be a movie about cancer).

Must.

Ought.

Have to.

The expectations projected on to our "miracle marriage" can feel suffocating.

Scripture only mentions Lazarus's sisters. It's silent as to whether or not Lazarus had a wife, but I'm willing to bet that after Orpheus rescued her from Hades, Eurydice feared she was going to be expected to be a Proverbs 31 woman, putting out and going down with gusto every night. Part of me suspects Eurydice was relieved that Orpheus lost his nerve and turned around too soon to see her, sending his beloved back into the shadows. The dead don't speak, but the oughts don't speak to the dead anymore either. The only ones immune to the oughts' accusations are those below ground.

Paul also says that oughts only elicit the opposite of their intent. Everyone already knows this to be true of children. As soon as you tell a kid they ought to eat their vegetables, they're determined not to eat them. The mistake grown-ups make is in thinking we're much different when it comes to relationships. In terms of relationships, the oughts make the marital bed quicksand. The more you get hung up on the musts and should of what your marriage ought to be, the more mired your marriage will become in your mutual HPtFTU. *You ought to be more patient* produces more impatience. *You should be more kind* chips away at whatever kindness already exists. *We must make love more* will mean more lonely nights or beating the bishop in the shower. The philosopher Alain de Botton echoes Paul's point when he says: "There is nothing more sterile than the demand to be constantly exciting."[1]

The oughts always accuse.

For my money, it's existentially obvious regardless of what you believe about Jesus or his resurrection.

The reason I think HPtFTU is a solid replacement for sin is because we, thanks to errant Christian sanctimony, tend to think of *sin* as the bad things that bad people do. But, in fact, Paul sees sin as the good that good people do when they think they have something they need to prove. Sin is more often what we do whenever we attempt to justify ourselves by our goodness. In doing so, we invariably eff things up along the way. The prodigal kid with his profligate living, then, isn't as much a sinner by this standard as his elder prick of a brother who's smug and satisfied in the certainty that he's earned his standing in the family.

So forget two kids who shag out of wedlock and think of Ali and me a decade and a half into our wedlock. To live in sin is to listen to the oughts accuse you for who and what you and your spouse aren't. Contrary to how we use the now-quaint cliché about living in sin, no one lives in sin more than two people who listen to the oughts accuse them that their marriage *should* be different or better, sexier, more fulfilling or less on fire with their mutual human propensity to fuck things up. And according to Paul's merciless logic, no one lives in more sin than do two people who mistakenly think their marriage must merit their miracle: a groom and a bride who believe their life together ought to justify their reprieve from death.

THE BACKASSWARDS PROMISE OF THE GOSPEL

Private Ryan didn't owe anything to anyone. His debt had already

---

1. Alain de Botton, ed., *On Being Nice* (London: The School of Life, 2017), 13.

been paid. It'd been paid in the currency of Christ himself, once for all. I realize how preachy that sounds, but take it from me. Shit, take it from Ali. Some of the stained-glass language that gets said in the pulpit can save you in the bedroom. Grace, says Paul, frees us from the demands of the oughts, and, more importantly, grace alone fulfills the demands of those oughts, creating what ought can only command.

If this book is the closest you've been to church in a while, consider this your crib note. By *grace*, Christians refer to God prodigally reckoning Christ's own faithfulness to you, gratis. His perfect score is forever your permanent record—and your spouse's. The backasswards promise of the gospel of grace is that by his own faithfulness Christ purchased each of us out of obligation. We don't need to earn anything anymore.

The language of scorekeeping is always forevermore antithetical to grace.

Despite how it's read ad nauseam at weddings, Paul's familiar love song in 1 Corinthians 13 is only achievable when the bride and groom trust that by love Paul means *Jesus*. He's talking about Jesus. "Jesus is patient, Jesus is kind, Jesus is not envious or boastful or arrogant or rude. Jesus does not insist on his own way."

Grace, to put the hypothesis bluntly, makes every couple's relationship a three-way and holds out the possibility that every married pair might be a parable of a love not of their own doing.

Grace is the good news that no one is keeping score; therefore, grace says that there's no expectation you need to fulfill, no measurement you need to meet. You and your beloved don't need to keep up with the Joneses or your childhood illusions of wrinkle-free, wedded bliss. Grace says there's no storybook marriage you two need to write together because the ledger book has been thrown out the window for good.

Grace frees you, in other words, to be ordinary. And, in a world of accusing oughts, any married couple will know, miracle or not, that's extraordinary.

In *We Learn Nothing*, cartoonist Tim Kreider reflects on his own brush with death, having been stabbed in the throat. After first observing the obvious ("We only notice we're alive when we're reminded we're going to die, the same way some of us appreciate our girlfriends only after they've become exes"), Kreider goes on to note how fleeting and impermanent is our grasp of grace: "You can't feel crazily grateful to be alive your whole life any more than you can stay passionately in love forever—or grieve forever, for that matter. Time makes us all betray ourselves and get back to the busywork of living."[2]

Kreider is probably correct, but perhaps the rare menace in my marrow makes Ali and me the rare exception to the rule. It's harder for time to make you a traitor to yourself when your days are like sand in a smaller-than-average hourglass. Living with uncertainty as I do, I can't get enough comfortable distance on my reprieve to fall completely back into the busyness of life. Like the tides, each new moon reminds me of my mortality as rudely as a cross traced in ash on my forehead.

Every month I come to be pricked and prodded and to sit on a vinyl table covered in butcher paper where I stare at a copy of my latest blood report, and I wonder where on the bell curve I'll fall and how much time I've got left on the vow that puts it too polite by half. The schedule on my fridge door says "Maintenance Chemo," but I've come to think of them as appointments with grace. I come and I get stuck and I watch the bag of poison scrunch and wrinkle as it empties into me its promise of life for a little longer, and I'm reminded again that my life now—same as before—is grace, a gift I do not deserve. Every IV that puts the poison in me extracts the venom of expectation and quiets the oughts' accusation that Ali and I need to be something other than the broken but committed lovers we are.

No sooner has my monthly reminder of my mortality given me my fix, heightening my awareness to the grace to which I've oth-

2. Tim Kreider, *We Learn Nothing: Essays* (New York: Simon & Schuster, 2013), 3.

erwise grown numb, then I'm off the wagon and relapsing back into thinking I need to work to make my life and my marriage merit my miracle. Just as the chemo nausea fades after a while, I'm quickly back to believing "earn this," that my marriage with Ali ought to meet all the measure of perfection others project on it.

Jonathon died on Good Friday.

I got the word as I pulled into the church parking lot for an evening Tenebrae service. When I got home, after the last candle was snuffed out and the altar stripped bare, I told Ali the news.

We cried and we hugged and we kissed.

And then, with the kids away at friends' houses, we did more.

I didn't suck in my stomach or hide the lube in my hand or try to stay hard for any superhero *50 Shades* lengths.

We left the lights on and the door irresponsibly ajar.

We kept our eyes open.

And, with the dogs both barking, we said "I love you" with sighs too deep for words.

Still, I can't say whether we did it because we both wanted it or because, hearing of Jonathon, we felt like that's what we, with two feet in the grave, ought to do.

CHAPTER 2.

JUNK IN THE TRUNK

A man cleaves to his wife and they become one flesh.
> —from The Book of Common Prayer

St. Paul never said: "While we were yet sinners, Christ died for us, on the condition that after a reasonable length of time we would be the kind of people no one would ever have had to die for in the first place. Otherwise the whole deal is off."
> —Robert Capon, *Between Noon and Three*

BAD SANTA

"I've always had a thing for Santa Claus. It's like a deep-seated childhood thing."

"So's my thing for tits."

Ali laughed, as she always does, at Billy Bob Thornton's line in the movie *Bad Santa*. You can hear that she's from Iowa when her laugh is genuine: it's loud and loose, not anxious at all. Ali laughed at Billy Bob Thornton's lecherous shopping-mall Santa, took a sip of her wine, and passed me a string of lights.

Almost a year from when our nightmare had begun, it was ending. As sprouts of hair cropped up along my receding hairline and a feeling of normalishness returned to my body so did a nearly forgotten sense of hopefulness visit our family.

I checked: for both of us, Ali and me, it felt like we were waking groggily from a nightmare and entering a dream. Sure, to anyone else the dream might seem domestic and dull, filled with dirty dishes in the sink, dog hair ground down in the floorboards, and boy pee splatted on the toilet seats. For us, it was the kind of dream you have while taking a crisp-fall-afternoon nap or after you've made love in the early morning and have fallen back asleep with the window open. We were entering the sort of dream that makes you want to draw the shades and curl up in the comforter. It was the sort of fantasy where some part of your sleeping self knows you're dreaming and so tries to manipulate the illusion in order to make it come out the way you hope.

Coming out of the crucible of stage-serious chemo and, now, living with incurable cancer, everyone wanted to talk to me about perspective. *Jason, you must really appreciate the little things now, the things that really matter*, people project onto me. And it's not that I don't appreciate every freaking minute of my reprieve, but the assumption that I must do so has a way of endowing every damn moment with an IMPORTANCE that feels like an accusation. No one wants to find a death exoneree scratching his balls and frittering away the hours watching *Seinfeld* reruns. In the same way, surviving (for now) cancer left me thinking I had to constantly be making scrapbook-worthy memories, that every minute of the time I didn't know I'd have had to be a Precious Moments kind of moment lest I was guilty of wasting the gravy time I'd been given.

I approached our first post-chemo Christmas with the unreflective expectation that this would be one of the memories that eventually flashes before my eyes. Maybe it's obvious; it wasn't to me: no spouse should have to bear such a burden. No child can. I anticipated that Christmas the way I had when our boys were little and believed in myths and miracles. The angel's summons, "You shall call him Emmanuel, which means God-with-us," would ring truer to me, I assumed, after long stretches of time when God's presence and with-ness had been an open question.

One of the ways I'd determined to have a meaningful, IMPORTANT, Precious Moments kind of Christmas was by decorating the Christmas tree, a task that as a pastor at a busy time of the work year had always felt like an afterthought. I brought to the $50 tree from Home Depot the same Survivor's Scrapbook intentionality I felt compelled to bring to every domestic ritual. To Sufjan Steven's Christmas album, my boys strung shiny blood-red beads on the branches and set out the many creepy faceless angels I've been given by parishioners over the years. Ditto the nativity sets and Advent calendars (some of which, I noticed for the first time, featured pigs, which I'm fairly certain did not grace the manger of the Jewish Messiah).

Ali and I put the boys to bed with the tree half decorated, thinking it would be romantic to finish decorating it together. I don't mean romantic in a *Love Actually* kind of way or romantic-sexy the way Nicolette Scorsese appears in visions to Chevy Chase in *Christmas Vacation*. I just thought it would be romantic in an IMPORTANT moment kind of way to drink a glass of wine and decorate the Christmas tree while we watched our favorite Christmas movie, *Bad Santa*.

If you haven't seen *Bad Santa*, in which a boozing, skirt-chasing shopping-mall Santa grifts his way into the home of a little boy and the senile grandma stewarding him, then please don't watch it until after you've read this book. You'll only judge me. Both of us love *Bad Santa* for the way it pops the pretensions of Christmas and tells the truth about how screwed up family can be, albeit in a profane and exaggerated way. Still, the movie manages to pull off the right kind of tender and to tell the truth about whatever the Gospel writer must've meant by announcing that in Christ, God put on sin and skin and lived among people just like us.

I thought it would be a romantic evening because it's one of our favorite movies—we serve and volley lines from it all year round. Whenever our boys bring home their report cards, Ali or I will steal a glance and mouth to the other: "Shit kid, I never got any D's." Or whenever one of them pouts and acts disappointed, we reply like Billy Bob Thornton to Thurman Merman: "Well, they can't all be winners, can they?" And when of our boys begs us for something, after they've stomped off scowling, we'll giggle to the other: "Shit in one hand, kid, and wish in the other. See which fills up faster."

Sometimes we don't even need to say the line. We can read it in the other's smiling eyes.

The stage was set that Advent night to be IMPORTANT and scrapbooked immediately upon completion. I'd uncorked the wine. We'd laughed—belly laughed—at the lewdest scenes in the movie. And now, post-chemo and recently once again sufficiently virile to deliver the goods myself, we were aglow, grateful to be alive. But for some reason, I was not being Precious Moments tender or intentional at all.

I was being a total dick.

I hung ornaments—ones we'd bought together or the kids had made—with the vacant affect of a zombie. I kept leaving the room to wash dishes that didn't need washing right then or to wipe down counters still wet and soapy from the last time I'd wiped them. When Ali said we needed to string more lights, I heard it as a complaint, a tremor of an outburst waiting to quake. When she pointed to a bare spot on the tree, I sighed like a martyr and whisper-shouted, "Okay!" or "Sorry!" as though she were pissed and had screamed at me.

Another funny scene came on the screen, but Ali didn't laugh. I saw a tear rolling down her cheek.

"This isn't fair, Jason. You do this every Christmas. It's like you're living in a completely different home, with different people—none of whom is *me*." And it *wasn't* fair. It was IMPORTANT, but not in the way I'd planned to orchestrate for the night.

I'd told Ali the stories of my parents and my family and our not-pleasant holidays; I'd told them to her back when we were dating but far enough into our relationship that I trusted her not to bail on me. She knew the stories, but she didn't know how right she was in that moment. I was in a different home next to a different Christmas tree, stuck there because of the words I still refused to trust.

POTATO CHIPS WITH A MILK CHASER

The same year my dad hit the tree in our driveway, ripping an ugly gash in its trunk by my swing, my grandpa came for a rare visit on Christmas Eve. My mother was working the night shift at the hospital, and I suspect my grandpa was there to keep an eye on my father after the tree incident and others like it that year. Throughout my parents' marriage, my grandfather occasionally made unannounced, short-lived attempts at drying my father out. He never said as much, and he never took him for any type of treatment. He would just show up and, for example, take my dad fishing for the weekend.

My grandpa was there with my sister and me on Christmas Eve. We had finished up the dishes when my father came home from whatever bar had closed early for the holiday. He was quite drunk. There were Christmases when he'd never come home at all, but he'd never come home drunk on Christmas. He was amiable despite his state, joking around with my younger sister. He was slurring some joke to her when he reached into the refrigerator for milk. He then took a bag of potato chips from the cupboard. I was watching television with my grandpa, neither of us acknowledging his drunkenness, when my father came over to the couch with potato chips and milk in hand. He matter-of-factly poured the milk into the potato-chip bag. I imagine this seemed perfectly natural to him because he then reached into the bag to eat the milk-sodden chips. I remember my grandpa looking away from the TV screen to raise an eyebrow at my father.

"He's just joking around for you," I told my sister. "Right dad?" He stared over at her with a glazed smile and slurred "Liiiiisssssa" with a sedate tone of reassurance.

A year or so later, after my dad had disappeared for a couple of days, I remember my mom driving me around town to help her look for his car. Finding one that looked like it, she had me get out and peer inside to make sure. His Lionel Ritchie and Genesis cassettes sat on the console next to a lighter and the Huey Lewis and the News *Sports* album. He was parked in front of a town home. It was Christmastime.

I can remember the colored lights on whoever's porch reflecting on my mom's windshield.

After my parents finally split up for good, Christmas got a different kind of chaotic for us. My mom struggled knowing that we weren't having the sort of Christmas she thought we ought to have, the Christmas she thought other families gave their children. The oughts always accuse, and this ought stressed her out. Disappointed her. Frustrated her.

Every year it would come to a head while we decorated the Christmas tree. Every year, trimming the tree invariably ended with me shouting unfair accusations and shedding tears and my mom throwing the treetop angel on to the floor and yelling "To hell with it all!" One Christmas she pushed the artificial tree down on its side just as the jack-in-box from the stop-motion *Rudolph the Red-Nosed Reindeer* said, "We're all misfits."

GHOSTS FROM CHRISTMASES PAST

"This isn't fair, Jason. You do this every Christmas. It's like you're living in a completely different home, with different people—none of whom is *me*."

The angel for the tree was on the floor where she'd thrown it, her voice stretched taut like it gets when she's defending one of our boys to a teacher. A blush crept up her throat. She looked as though she were having an allergic reaction to this version of me.

We should've been watching a Jason Bourne movie rather than *Bad Santa*. Getting shot with chemo-poison and living when you'd expected to die is like waking up slowly from amnesia and discovering who you really are and not liking everything you find. Ali had opened the safe-deposit box where I hid my other passports from myself. Throwing the angel down, she triggered a film strip of memories that came flooding back to me, memories that had formed me.

When people tell me, as they often do, that my illness must have given me new perspective on my life, they're more correct than they likely would ever guess. It wasn't until I woke up in this liminal space, in between the nightmare of stage-serious cancer and the dream of maybe more years ahead, that I was able to perceive the extent to which I'd never left that home of my childhood.

Here's what I know as a pastor: to some extent or another, incurable cancer or no cancer at all, we never leave our childhood homes behind. It's why, I think, no one is ever truly ready for marriage. I say it all the time in my wedding sermons, but weddings are about the worst time and place for a sermon (or advice giving). No one remembers a single thing the preacher says, especially the bride and groom.

I dated Ali for eight years before we got married. If it was possible for any couple to be ready for marriage, it would've been us. We knew each other, trusted each other, and had grown up together. We had a solid friendship and shared values upon which to build a marriage. We had the blessing of our families and the encouragement of our friends. Still, we weren't ready for marriage because *nobody's ready for marriage*. Marriage is a covenant of trust, intimacy, fidelity, and self-sacrifice forever. No one is ready for a covenant like that until they're thrust into the middle of it and forced to find their way in the dark.

Only marriage makes you ready for marriage, for only a life

lived with another can illumine how, in many ways, you're still stuck living in the home whence you came.

Like muscle memory, hanging the ornaments, stringing the lights, topping the tree, it all conjured up the chaos I'd experienced as a kid. As a consequence, it drew out of me old anxieties, put me on edge, primed me to watch every movement of Ali's body language and listen for every inflection in her voice, braced to anticipate and thereby prevent a blow up. Of course, I'd provoked exactly what I'd wanted to avoid: another Christmas Eve with the treetop angel thrown on the floor.

Maybe this is the only kind of cheating where just one person is to blame.

"You do this every Christmas" she'd rightly screamed at me. I never noticed I did it every Christmas until after I thought I'd have no Christmases left. I never realized how much junk I'd trucked into our marriage. Only after my reprieve did I learn how my refusal to trust Christ's words repeated itself in my relationship with Ali.

When the Bible talks about marriage in the old King James translation, it uses an odd but illuminating word. It says a man and woman will cleave from their mothers and fathers and will cleave to one another.

Cleave is one of those insanely illogical yet strangely efficient words with two mutually exclusive definitions.

Cleave:

1. To split or sever, especially along a natural grain.

2. To stick fast to, adhere.

Cleave is the word Scripture most often uses to describe what God wants us to do by being married. We're supposed to sever ourselves from our family of origin and stick fast to the new family our marriage creates.

We're meant to cleave and then to cleave.

Before cancer began to kill me, *cleave* had always proved a convenient back-pocket counseling tool for couples prior to their nuptials. "What habits or practices from your families of origin do you want to bring into your new family," I'd ask, more curious about the clause to come, "and what do you want to leave behind?" Usually the glassy-eyed grooms and brides-to-be would volunteer something along the lines of how they wanted to have ham on Easter instead of lamb or how they didn't want to repeat the pattern of the Dad who never vacuumed.

"I don't want us to fight on Christmas Eve like my parents always used to," one future Mrs. told me like she was on a mission from the future to rescue me. Ignoring her, I transitioned to the compatibility tests my denomination has me administer to the engaged. Apart from Ali tossing the treetopper on the floor while Billy Bob Thornton licked his lips over Mrs. Santa's Helper's bosom, I don't know that I would've appreciated how the King James's use of *cleave* connotes more than a family's Christmas traditions.

We bring into marriage more than our dad's opinion on whether the forks should point up or down in the dishwasher. Like the ticket stubs that get left and forgotten as bookmarks, we also bring into our marriage the scores we've not settled and the scabs we've picked at so many times they've never fully healed. Maybe when Christ urges us to cleave from, for marriage, he has in mind those other words he was dying to tell us: "You are forgiven." Marriage makes me wonder if what gets the begrudgers' goat when Jesus declares "You are forgiven" is that he's not declaring the forgiveness of the sins they've *committed* but forgiveness for the sins they've *held onto*, the grievances as precious as the photos you'd rush into a burning house to rescue. Maybe what makes them irate isn't the letting go by God of what they've done to others but the letting go of what has been done to them by others.

Like my mom and her dad before her, I've perpetuated the family habit of falling asleep at night, reading on the sofa, a glass of wine between my legs and a book on my lap, long after I've been told to come to bed. Before we bind ourselves to another, we're to let go of the sins sinned against us, to let go of the ways people have damaged us, as people have a propensity to do. We've got to cleave when we leave our families and cleave to a new one, God says. We've got to let go of the gripes and grievances we're still gripping in pride or protest. There is now no condemnation, Paul insists without leaving any air for argument. The Father has let go of all sins, including the ones we're still holding onto.

With Ali fighting back tears and yelling at me, my unsightly, unvarnished first response was to get angry at her. To fight back. To justify why I was being a prick and had apparently been so every Christmas since we married. I had to bite my lip to keep from shouting. My nails left marks in my palms so tight had I began to clench my hands—not out of any urge to do violence but out of my righteousness.

My rightness.

Turns out that word *cleave* isn't just odd. It's offensive. The offense is grace. Because here's the rub: you may have a very good reason to be holding onto your grievances. It's no wonder we go looking for better words than grace and find, "You can forgive but you can't forget" an attractive alternative.

Like the nail marks in my palms, here's another sensation I noticed standing next to the Christmas tree. I *wanted* to be pissed off at Ali. The self-rightness and aggrieved anger felt good. It sure as hell felt better than trying to conceive, as I attempted later, how I would swallow my indignant pride and forget and forgive. For a split second, I even wondered what life would be like if I left her or she me. I was so loath to let go of my hurts that I considered, for just a moment by the Christmas tree, letting go of my love and leaving my marriage. Surely, this is the most original of sins.

In *We Learn Nothing*, Tim Kreider notices how anger works in our bodies like lust or opiates. He speculates that the real reason we revel in righteous anger is because "it spares us from the impotent pain of empathy, and the harder, messier work of understanding."[1] It's easier, more enjoyable even, to be justified by our anger than it is to be justified by another. What Ali helped me to see was that I wasn't just holding on to the sins sinned against me. The sins sinned against me defined me. From childhood on up, I was the product of my parent's brokenness, and I didn't want to let go of those scars. Who would I be without them? I'd invested a lot of my self-image in the sob story I rehearsed for you a few pages ago. I was the son of a deadbeat drinking dad, who'd overcome the odds thrown at him and blah, blah, blah. I was the child of a mother who parentified me prematurely by forcing me to find my father out in the arms of another yada, yada, yada. Overcoming my upbringing had earned me a kind of righteousness. The scabs it left behind, I thought, merited me sympathy, certainly from others, definitely from Ali, and maybe from God too.

Because my eyes had been shut in righteous indignation, I couldn't see how my parents, too, were the products of imperfect parents also afflicted with the propensity to screw things up.

The sympathy I thought I was owed kept me from the empathy I owed to my parents. But Kreider is right about it being hard and messy; it doesn't come as easy as that last sentence. To have your identity determined not by your wounds but by Christ's wounds, to say "I forgive you" because *all is forgiven* is to feel as naked as Jesus upon the cross.

EMMAUS AT THE BASS PRO SHOPS

I went to see my mom after Christmas. Even before the angel incident with Ali, my relationship with my mom had hit a snag. Even in the most litigious of families, there comes a point where the juice is no longer worth the squeeze and you stop arguing.

1. Tim Kreider, *We Learn Nothing: Essays* (New York: Simon & Schuster, 2013), 49.

But since fighting is all you know how to do, you stop talking altogether.

That's the place my mom and I now inhabited.

She'd sent me a message: "Let's meet for dinner somewhere."

I replied back to her, "Sure," and I suggested a couple dates and asked for a destination. She sent back only an address. A seemingly random place along Interstate 95. I didn't even try to find it on a map. I replied again, "Okay."

And then with much sarcasm and equal parts cynicism, I entered the date in my iPhone calendar along with the title: "Reconciliation Dinner."

The day of, I typed the address into Google Maps and a hundred miles later it announced that my destination was on my left. I slowed the car, stared to the side, and concluded that my mom must be punking me.

Because there on my left was Bass Pro Shops.

It's a manure-colored structure that stretches as far as the eye can see. In case you're unfamiliar, Bass Pro Shops is a shopping mall exclusively for hunting and fishing.

Imagine if Costco sold only blueberry muffins and you have an idea of the scale and specificity that is Bass Pro Shops. Let's just say, if it's not already obvious, I'm not really a Bass Pro Shops kind of guy.

I was afraid that to call and question the choice of meeting places would only provoke another argument, so I got out of the car and walked the two miles through the parking lot to the store, all the while feeling like a tribute in *Hunger Games* headed toward the Cornucopia. Like a lumberjack of yore, I walked through the heavy, fake-timbered front doors and then pushed my waist through a turnstile.

If Virginia is a red-leaning state, then I think it fair to say that the Bass Pro Shops in Richmond is like the spot on the planet Jupiter: super-red. For example, after I walked through the turnstile, to my left, where you might expect a coat check at a swankier establishment, customers were checking their concealed handguns.

"Did you bring a weapon with you, sir?" the greeter asked me.

"Weapon? Uh, just these," I said, holding up my hands.

He kinked his eyebrow as though he was thinking there's no way you could stand your ground with hands of such unimpressive caliber. I stood there, staring back over at the gun check.

"Are you looking for something, sir?" he asked.

"Um, I was just wondering where I can tie up my horse," I joked.

He didn't laugh. You could tell it struck him like a good idea. I'd gotten there early. I had time to kill, and I still had birthday shopping to do for my son, so I wandered the store. After a while, another employee asked me if she could help me.

"Yeah, do you sell fishing poles here?"

She looked at me with the sort of empathy one reserves for stroke patients and pointed in the direction behind her. I walked past ladies camouflage lingerie, Duck Dynasty onesies, and "Gun Control Means Using Two Hands" outdoor thermostats. Finally I happened upon not simply a fishing section but an entire forest of fishing poles. And behind it, hidden like a high-stakes baccarat table, was an entire fly-fishing section.

I browsed, and every now and then I would let out a manly grunt like I knew what I was looking at. Eventually I let myself get taken advantage of and I bought Gabriel a boy's fly rod and reel and then, checking the time, I hiked back to the front of the store to meet my mom.

I stood outside next to a deer-hunting stand and waited for her. We said hi and walked inside and stepped through the turnstile.

"Do you have any weapons with you?" the same greeter asked her.

"Just these two," I said again, and he rolled his eyes at me.

It turns out that in addition to a two-story waterfall and a day-care center for your dogs, the Bass Pro Shops also has a full-service restaurant and bar in it.

The restaurant was decorated like a swampy alligator Applebee's. Captain Sig Hansen from *Deadliest Catch* was catching something on the flat screen over the bar. The hostess sat us awkwardly in the middle of the dining room where we were surrounded by a busload of elderly ladies and a high-school cheerleading squad.

At first we tested the temperature before we tiptoed too far into conversation: nice to see you, how are you, what's new with you, how are the boys?

We must've looked like we were deep in conversation. Because when the waitress came over to take our drink order, she apologized for interrupting us.

As the waitress walked away, my mom said, "I'm sorry . . . for everything."

"Me too," I said.

And then we got down to the brass tacks of what each of us was sorry for.

After a while, the waitress brought us the glasses of wine we'd ordered along with a loaf of bread on a wooden cutting board. Probably because it gave us something else to say, something safely rote and memorized, we said grace. We didn't hold hands or make a show of it or anything. We just quietly said grace.

And having blessed the bread, I took it. And because the waitress forgot to leave us a knife, I broke the bread. Into two pieces. And I gave the bread to my mom.

That way of putting it makes me sound like the Easter Jesus on the way to Emmaus rather than him being host to both of us, present to us in the words we were trying to trust: "I forgive you."

In our appetite for bad news, we not only refuse to trust God's words, we refuse to see the God who speaks those unequivocal words of forgiveness. *PS*, Paul says, *that means there is now no condemnation. Nothing can separate you from the love of God.*

Around the same time I met my mom at the Bass Pro Shops, my dad had a heart attack.

I flew up to Cleveland when I got the call.

He almost died.

My dad and me—we have a history. Our relationship has been complicated and tense and . . . sticky, the way it always is in a family when addiction and infidelity and abuse are part of the story.

Some hurts never go away. Some scores never get settled.

Unless you have faith that all scores have been settled, once for all.

A few days after his heart attack, my dad went home. We were sitting in his garden, just him and me and my stepmom. My dad's face was black. His nose was broken from where he'd fallen on the street. His chest was sore. His breathing was tight from the CPR.

My dad and me, we don't have the kind of relationship where we know how to just sit in the garden with each other—if you know what I mean.

So we were sitting there and it wasn't long before he started picking at me. Picking at old wounds. Picking old fights.

He'd nearly died. And he just wanted to go back at it.

I thought: *Really, you want to do this now? Right here?*

But it didn't take long for me to take the bait, and there I was arguing twenty-year-old resentments with my nearly dead dad.

We didn't get very far though. A couple of moments. A couple of raised voices.

And then my stepmom (she's the born-again type) stood up, gestured in the middle of us, and scolded: "Whatever you think is between you, it's gone. It's not here anymore."

And then she pointed at me or, rather, the cross on my neck and said: "I expect you, at least, to understand that."

Not only did I not understand what she meant (about sins

being gone, gratis), I didn't appreciate how she'd also just given me quite possibly the very best marriage advice.

I wonder—do we persist in imagining that God is at the end of his rope because there are plenty of people with whom we're at the end of ours? But if you believe that God in Jesus Christ is unconditionally *for us*, then you've also got to believe that you should not hold anything against someone else. If you believe that God in Christ Jesus refuses to condemn you, then you've got to believe that it should be ditto for the people in your life. And if you believe that nothing can separate us from the love of God in Christ Jesus, nothing in all creation, then you must also believe, or at least be willing to attempt to believe, that because of the love of God in Christ Jesus, then nothing can separate us from one another.

Of course, if it were easy to love like Jesus, we wouldn't need Jesus.

Maybe the best we can do is imitate the father who proclaims, "Lord, I believe; help my unbelief."

A few nights later, after the tree had been thrown out to the curb and the trimmings put back in their boxes and taken to the basement, I laid in the dark next to Ali in bed. "I'm sorry," I said, without needing to add any explanatory whats or whys.

"I forgive you," she said.

We held each other as tight as Mary Magdalene tries to hold onto the Easter Jesus in the garden.

"Noli me tangere" Jesus says to Mary in the Latin of John's Gospel. "Do not hold on to me." As much as she'd like, she can't hold on to him. She has to let go. All her sins are in him. She has to cleave. That Mary could not hold on to Jesus made me hold Ali harder than maybe I ever had before in our marriage. It might also have been the first night of my life I had gone to bed a believer.

We lay like that in bed for so long that I was nearly asleep when

Ali spoke into the darkness, "You know, why do we need a live tree that needs decorating every Christmas?"

"What? We can't not have a Christmas tree, honey."

"No, I mean why don't we get one of those pre-lit hipster tinsel trees for next Christmas?"

"Don't those cost a fortune?" I asked, rolling over so that I was the inside spoon.

"They're not cheap, no," she replied. "But I think it's worth it."

"But you've always had a live tree," I said. "I don't want you to give that up."

"It's not giving anything up," she said. "It's starting something different."

CHAPTER 3.

THAT'S WHAT SHE SAID

The condition of Man after the fall of Adam is such, that he cannot turn and prepare himself, by his own natural strength and good works, to faith.

—Article X of the Articles of Religion,
The First Book of Common Prayer (1549)

VITAMIX JESUS

Back before the Risen Jesus knocked his ass blind, Paul bussed tables for the begrudgers. He stood by and handed the lynch mob the rocks to stone Stephen. After Paul was nursed back to health, he became a new and changed man, from persecutor to apostle, disregarding his resume and former life as no better than a steaming pile of *skubala*, shit.

After I was nursed back from near death to life (for now), I proved to be less like the apostle and more like the beautiful house in that Talking Heads song. Same as it ever was.

At best, I'm a Paul who'd hand Stephen's stoners smaller rocks.

Since maintenance chemo is a quick way to blow through a copay in an afternoon, Ali and I had committed to spend less and save more. When I say "we'd committed to spend less and save more," I mean, of course, that I'd nodded yes when Ali asked me if I would promise to stop spending money on crap and stupid shit. If you're unclear as to the fine, wine-like distinctions between crap on the one hand and stupid shit on the other, then you can ask Ali for clarification. I suspect the camouflage Snuggie I'd bought her for Valentine's Day (as a gag gift) would qualify as crap while the Gandalf staff and robe I purchased (for me) at the Renaissance Festival, for upwards of a car payment, would count, specifically so, as stupid shit.

Attempting to heed my promise to change my spending habits, in the months after my recovery I had avoided what for me has the same siren-song pull that porn has upon lesser men: TV infomercials. I'm a complete sucker for infomercials. A pushover, Ali would say. An easy mark.

For example, if I was surfing the channels and I heard the words "set it and forget it" fuggedaboutit, I was hooked, convinced I absolutely needed to be able to rotisserie six chickens at one time. If I was flipping channels and came across the infomercial for the Forearm Max, I'd spend the next two hours shamefully amazed that I've made it this far in my life with forearms as pathetic as mine. If I saw the commercial for the Shake Weight, my first thought was never "That seems to simulate something that violates the book of Leviticus." No, my first thought was always, "That looks like something I need."

To that end, I suggested to Ali that we cut the cord and get rid of our cable, thereby evicting the pusher from my crack den of crap. A brave suggestion, I thought, using it as an occasion to imagine myself as Gene Hackman in the *Poseidon Adventure*, the wise-cracking clergyman who risks his life for the otherwise doomed crew. (Only later did I consider that Gene Hackman's character doesn't survive in the film.)

Like Gene Hackman's character, I should've realized that Gabriel and I were sunk the moment we went to get some fish at the market. At that point, I'd been on the infomercial wagon for three months, two weeks, and four days. But guess what I discovered they were doing back by the seafood section? That's right, a product demonstration.

The person doing the demonstration was a woman in her twenties or thirties. For some inexplicable, yet very effective reason she was wearing a black evening dress that reminded me of the one worn by Angelina Jolie in *Mr. & Mrs. Smith.*

"Hey, let's stick around and watch this," I said to Gabriel, who smacked his forehead with here-we-go-again embarrassment.

In addition to the slinky dress, the demonstrator was wearing a Madonna mic, which pumped her bedroom voice through speakers, beckoning all the men in the store to obey her siren call. The product she was demonstrating that day was the Vitamix. If you never recovered from the stock market crash of 2008, then you might not know that the Vitamix is like the Bentley of blenders.

Angelina pulled the Vitamix out of its box like a jeweler at Tiffany's. And then she went into her schtick: "The Vitamix is a high-powered blending machine for your home or your office. It's redefining what a blender can do. The Vitamix will solve all your blending problems. With this one product, you won't need any of those other tools and appliances taking up so much space in your kitchen."

And as she spoke, I wasn't thinking: Who needs a high-powered blender for their office? Why does a blender need redefining? It's just a blender. If space is the issue in your kitchen, then is a blender with more horsepower than a Prius really the solution?

No, I was thinking, This could solve all my blending problems. If I have this, I won't need anything else.

I looked down at my side; whether because he likes to cook or because he was nearing puberty, Gabriel was transfixed too.

The first part of her demo, she showed off the Vitamix's many juicing and blending capabilities. But then to display the diversity of the product's features, she asked the crowd, "Who enjoys pesto?"

And like a brown-nosing boy, desperate to impress the teacher (the teacher he has a crush on), I raised my hand and spoke up: "I do. I am Italian after all."

And she smiled at me (*only* at me) and said: "I've always had a thing for Italians."

Aheh.

"Can you cook?" she asked me. And I nodded my head. Like Fonzie, too cool for words.

"Even better," she purred.

"I went to Princeton!" I volunteered like an overly eager forty-year-old virgin.

And then she pretended to be speaking to the entire crowd even though I knew she only cared about me.

"Have you ever noticed how the pesto you buy in the store never looks fresh? It's dark and oily."

And all of us nodded like Stepford Husbands.

"But when you try to make pesto at home"—and she held up her hands like this was a problem on par with AIDS or world hunger or Russian interference in our electoral process—"food processors and traditional blenders just won't do will they?"

And then she looked my way, like I was a plant in the audience. Hypnotized and dutiful and desperately wanting to do right by her, I said, "No, they won't do," even though I've been making pesto since I was ten years old, and I can't say I've ever had a problem.

She licked some of the pesto off her spoon as though it were a mansicle and then she said in her come-hither voice: "I'm not married (sigh) but if I was, this is what I'd want. From my husband. On Valentine's Day."

I drove my new Vitamix home that afternoon.

I showed it to Ali, presenting it to her like a hunter/gatherer laying his bounty at the foot of his lady's cave. And then I got right back in my car and drove it back to the store in order to return it.

I'd again broken my promise. It's a stupid, funny instance for sure. But, driving back to Whole Foods, I still loathed myself more than a little for failing to abide by the promise I'd made to her.

Ali just shook her head.

"You're an idiot," she said, rolling her eyes and kissing me on the neck. Not knowing I could see her as she walked away, I saw that she smiled.

And seeing her smile, I knew.

I knew I'd spend myself empty to keep being known like that and yet somehow still loved. The look on her face is often the only outward, visible sign of what I'm told God says about me. She's the sermon I need to hear. She's the only word that can quiet the contrary testimony of the hostile witness inside my head. And like most Sunday worshipers who step out of the sanctuary only to shake my hand and offer a perfunctory "that was interesting," I know I will never be able to convey adequately to my beloved how the word that she bears to me is the one word able to unbind me.

SPANK BANK

We can't have any more kids.

That's what you give up when you get stage-serious cancer. Likely, it's why the doctor asked if I wanted to spank off a sample before I started chemo. It left me infertile. Meanwhile, the incurable nature of my cancer left us ineligible to adopt. My survival odds make me a poor bet as an adoptive parent.

If we'd had another child, a daughter, then I like to think we would have named her after that word that Ali carries to me: Grace.

Grace is the Bible's name for unmerited, unexpected, one-way love.

It's ironic. We assume that it takes two to make a marriage work. We take it for granted that in order for a relationship to be loving, both partners must be investing love, actively so, into it.

Yet this is the opposite of how our relationship with God works. Why then should we suppose that our relationships with one another would work any different? Our relationship with the Beloved works by the operation of grace—one-way love—and so does, despite the assumptions, our relationship with our beloved.

Married couples rarely come to my office when their marriage is in a good place. That's a shame because—let's face it—it's when neither spouse is hostile, defensive, or bearing grudges that both of them are most likely to hear honest feedback. It's only in the absence of threat that people are willing to change their habits and try out new skills.

Nonetheless, like an overweight fifty-five-year-old who waits until it feels like an elephant is standing on his chest to go in for a routine checkup, most couples wait until their marriage is about five calories away from quadruple bypass to seek counseling. When couples wait that long, no matter the issues in their marriage, the conversation usually plays out the same way in my office. I feel like a referee at a tennis match, watching the accusations and hurt volleyed back and forth with neither willing to stop until someone declares the scorekeeping in their favor.

Marriages can get like that, tit for tat, tit for tat, tit for tat. The resentment and recriminations build until you feel powerless *not* to respond. The hurt becomes habituated, and before you know it the tit for tat has become your marital banter.

A lot of times couples stuck in the tit for tat will contend that they won't change until the other changes. While that may sound like equity and justice in another context, in the context of a marriage it's insanity. It's mutually assured destruction. And it's antithetical to the one-way love with which we're loved by God.

Contrary to the clichés—if grace is true, then for marriages stuck in a tit-for-tat spiral, it only takes one to begin the process of change and healing. That is, for marriages experiencing strain and sadness, marriages bowing under the weight of bad habits or burdensome expectations, healing can begin with only one spouse showing the other grace—undeserved, unexpected, one-way love.

One of the things I've learned about marriage, one of the things I've seen with my own eyes and in my own marriage, is that, yes it takes two to make a marriage, but it only takes one to start the process of healing and change. If grace is the way by which God rescues us from our sin, then such one-love is sufficient, too, to prime the pump, change the dynamic, and break the logjams in our own relationships.

Of course, Ali always gets her way so, rather than Grace, our daughter's name most likely would have been Elinor and spelled just that way.

"I'll do better," I said before I drove the Vitamix back to Whole Foods. The nimbus-like letters i-d-i-o-t still hung on in the air.

"Uh, huh," she said, still smiling (kind of).

"What? I will," I protested (too much).

"Jason, you can't even stop yourself from eating an entire jar of pickles once its opened."

It's true. Back when I was in the middle of one of my rounds of chemo, I had found an unopened jar of kosher dills hidden in the back of the fridge. I ate one. Then I quickly ate them all. I had done so innumerable times before. Only this time my white counts and blood chemistry were all out of whack. I instantly had the runs. Standing up from the toilet, my sodium level having gone from zero to a gazillion in an instant, I passed out on the bathroom floor.

"I'm pretty sure it's never a good idea to eat an entire jar of pickles," my oncologist offered the next day.

"But I love pickles so much."

If Ali were to wait for me to become what she graciously grants to me, then we'd need more time together than the bell curve wagers I've likely got left. Instead, thank God, she treats me as the husband I wish I were to her. As a pastor, it's always struck me as odd and ironic that when it comes to our relationship with

God, nearly every Christian and every non-Christian I've met will slam their fists and insist, as though their very lives are at stake (they are), that they have free will. Yet, when it comes to our closest approximation to our relationship with God, our relationships with our lovers, our everyday experience, invalidates what we insist is true about our Sunday Lover.

Whenever we speak of our bedmates, we use the passive voice. Something drew us together. I just knew she was the one. But whenever we speak of the God, we use, wrongly I'm told by Scripture, the active voice: I invited Christ into my heart. Come forward and give your life to God. I got (myself) saved. "I have decided to follow Jesus," sings the old hymn.

For both, our spouse and our savior, Stevie Ray Vaughan got it right: we're love struck, baby.

Every now and then I look at our prom picture, taken when we were both seventeen, young love blossoming just as OJ and Nicole's love ended in blood spray spattered on the carpet and Nancy Grace's nostrils splayed out across America's TV screens. In the picture, the seventeen-year-old staring back at me from my glossy prom picture can't be me. He just can't. He's wearing a painfully pinstriped tux, made of material cut from somewhere between Dick Tracy and Johnny Cash. Underneath, he's wearing an off-white, collarless dress shirt with a black onyx button—sort of like an outsized cuff link or a bolo tie minus the string, where the bow tie would go on a more sensible person. He can't be me, I think whenever I see him. Please, let it not be me.

The hair is fuller. The face is thinner. The frame not yet filled out, the eyes affecting a very deliberate Richard Gere–type squint (it was 1995) into Ali's own. Were it not for the presence of my future wife there in the photo, I might have plausible deniability, but instead all I have is gratitude that she married me in spite of my fashion crimes.

I don't know how the hell she fell in love with me. Having met on the high-school swim team, I like to joke that one look at me in a Speedo and she was a goner. But one look at the prom picture, and I know that's a lie. The only explanation is that I was her jar of pickles.

Nor do I know how I fell in love with Ali. I'm just self-aware enough to accede that I had as little volition over her effect on my heart as I do over a bag of Cheetos. I can never put away a bag with more than three Cheetos left in it. I'm also self-aware enough to know that I loved that she laughed at my jokes. I loved the freckles on her thighs, of which her swimsuit afforded me a glance, and I thought the muscles on her back as she swam were sexy.

But that's all hindsight at best and, in hindsight, I think "fell" is the exact word to use to describe the operation of love upon us. We stumbled upon and into each other's lives like hikers into a hole they did not dig, and then happily we discovered we rather liked it down there together.

If we acknowledge how we have so little agency of our own when it comes to the one who shares with us their body, then why are we so adamant to insist that we do so when it comes to the One who shares with us eternity? As professor of psychology Timothy Wilson puts it in his book *Strangers to Ourselves*: most of us make free, rational decisions less than one-fifth of the time.[1] The same invisible captivity that binds us to another's heart is what gets us to eat ourselves sick with Cheetos and pickles. It's what compels us to flirt with a girl in a cocktail dress in front of the fish monger.

No matter how adamant we are that we have free will, psychology confirms what Scripture contends and love songs know: we are not actually free. Incidentally, this is why so many Christian books of the advice type—Tips for a Happy, Healthy Marriage; Become a Better Beloved; Your Best Marriage Now—offer cold comfort. They are, as I've seen firsthand in the parish, cruel. We

---

1. Timothy Wilson, *Strangers to Ourselves: Discovering the Adaptive Unconscious* (Cambridge: Harvard University Press, 2004), 20.

already live in a world where oughts accuse us from all angles. Advice, as Robert Capon says, only adds to our lives the glide angle of a dump truck. It doesn't matter whether men are from Mars or women are from Venus because the more fundamental dilemma, according to the Bible generally and the New Testament specifically, is that every single refugee from Mars and Venus have their heads up Uranus. Any advice that assumes less is hokum.

Tips alone are no different than saying "Get down off your cross" to Christ. It assumes resurrection happens all on its own. Relationship advice alone is like telling a captive, "Free yourself! Pick the lock. Be your own chain-breaker and make your way through your wilderness." We need more than coaching or good counsel. Advice alone can't get us to love aright. We are people who need to be delivered. That neither mate in a marriage is truly free makes it all the more insane how we insist that love in a marriage must always be a reciprocal, two-way affair. Reciprocal love first requires redemption from captivity. And if the Bible is to be believed, only grace can set us free.

One-way love alone is the TNT that can break us free from the cages we can't see.

BORN-AGAIN SINNER

Take it from me, even a brush with death cannot scare us straight.

For a long time, I thought I was going to die. When I realized I wasn't going to die (yet), when I got my bone marrow results back and I realized the inevitable wasn't (yet), I was so freaking grateful. To God.

I felt so thankful that I promised a vow to God. For the gift of my life, I would offer the gift of my faithfulness. It's true. I stared at myself in the mirror at my oncologist's men's room right after I received my results. I splashed water on my face to make sure I wasn't daydreaming. I stared at myself in the mirror, and I swore that from here on out I would be a perfect Christian. No more snark or sarcasm. No more dark cynicism. No more cussing or anger. No more can't-be-bothered apathy or little white lies. God had rescued me from death. So I promised to the men's room mirror: "I will never sin again."

And I meant it.

And I did a pretty good job, until I walked out of the bathroom and over to the elevator. The elevator at my doctor's office, no matter the time of day, it's like the DMV was outsourced to supervise the Final Solution. It's a constipated, huddling mass of people frantic with their self-importance. So I waited and waited, as the elevator would come and close, come and close. Each time it was too crowded for me. But I was a good Christian. I kept my vow. I was patient. I did not think any dark thoughts in my heart. I did not sin.

So I was doing pretty good. My turn was next. I was right there at the front of the line. But as soon as the elevator doors opened, this old guy with wispy white hair and an oxygen mask, out of nowhere wedged a walker in between me and the elevator doors. And, like he was Patrick Ewing, he threw a varicosed elbow at me, pushing me out of the way to wait longer for another elevator.

He then looked at me as the elevator doors closed between us. And he smirked! And if anyone had been able to read my mind in that moment, I would've been whistled for a flagrant foul.

On my way home from the doctor, I stopped at Starbucks for a coffee. I was standing at the counter about to pay. Next to me, in front of the other register, a homeless man poured coins out of an empty bag of chips. Coming up short, he looked over at me. He asked if I had any money. Without thinking about it, without meaning to, just reflexively (which says a lot about me), I said: "I'm sorry, I don't have any cash." My words were still hanging thick in the air when I looked down at my wallet in my hand, which had a wad of wrinkled fives and tens sticking out of it like a bouquet of dirty green flowers. Not only had I lied, not only had I refused charity, I'd managed to lie to and stiff Jesus, who said whatever you do to the poor you've done it to him. Not to mention swearing false oaths is one of the Ten Commandments, so that was a sin too.

And leaving Starbucks, I accidentally cut a guy off in traffic. It was an accident, not a sin. But then when he rolled his window down to offer his opinion of me (at the traffic light), and when he offered his opinion of my mother (at the next light), and when he described everything he thought I deserved to do to myself (at the light after that), did I turn the rhetorical cheek? Did I forgive his trespass against me? Did I forgive him seventy times seven times? Did I offer to walk a mile in his jackass shoes?

No, I said goodbye to him with a sarcastic smile and a one-fingered wave.

On the way home, I made the mistake of going to the Soviet Safeway just down the road near my house. I was in the Express Line, the Fifteen Items or Less Line, behind this blue-haired woman who had twenty-eight items in her cart. Twenty-eight. I know because she was moving so slowly I had time to count the twenty-eight items in her cart at least twenty-eight times while we stood in the fifteen items or less aisle. But I didn't say anything. I didn't sigh out loud or point to the Express Line sign that she should've been able to see since it was nearly as big as her perm. No, I didn't complain. I didn't gripe that I had places to go and people to see. And I didn't complain when she pulled out a stack of wrinkled, mostly expired coupons to try to haggle the price down. No, I kept my vow. I was Jesusy good. But then when it came time to pay, the old lady reached in to a purse the size of El Salvador and after searching in it for, oh, I don't know, *forever*, what did she pull out?

That's right: a checkbook.

It was big and fat and had like eight rubber bands wrapped around it and old deposit slips sticking out everywhere. And after she then searched for her "favorite pen," she filled the check out like she was signing a Syrian Peace Treaty, and then she carefully tore the check out of the checkbook and then she marked the transaction down in her checkbook register with crossword puzzle care and then, finally, she handed the check to the teenager working the cash register, the teenager who had clearly never seen nor processed a check in his life.

"Oh my Lord! You should just keep a goat in that purse because the barter system would be a quicker way to pay!" I didn't say that to myself. God rescued me from death, and still my new life of sinless perfection—or just self-improvement—was shorter lived than a Trump White House staffer.

Later that evening when Ali got home, I told her about my vow and about how I could not even keep it as long as her work day. I didn't play any of it for yucks. She smiled at me anyway, tender not teasing, offering an unspoken, undeserved love that felt like a liberation.

"Of course you couldn't keep it. I know you. You're not exactly an enigma," she said, her head on my chest. She was hugging me. "I love you. Now make me dinner."

"Yes, ma'am."

WHILE WE YET SUCKED

Strike what I said earlier against advice-giving because here's some. But this isn't just marriage advice, it's *Christian* advice, advice on how to see other humans in light of the gospel. Here it goes: seeing others as Ali sees me, as bound and unfree, is the easiest way to find patience and empathy for others. It's when you mistakenly think people are free that you get pissed off at them. When you see people as active agents of everything in their lives, choosing the crap decisions they make, you can confuse what they do for who they are.

And I know this: you're just like me. You have your own Angelinas, your own jars of pickles, and your own bags of Cheetos you can't stay away from. You're not an enigma, but you have plenty of them in your life. Every spouse knows it already. The only consistent thing about you is your inconsistency. You're just like me.

The only fix for what ails us in our life with another is our willingness to receive and reciprocate a mercy that is as unmerited as it is unexpected, which means often it will stick in your craw, striking you as somewhere between uncomfortable and offensive.

When you vow "I do" to another, you are not promising "I can." You're not asserting an ability innate to you. Instead of the tit for tats that come so naturally to us, by your "I do" you're pledging your willingness to volley and serve a grace that comes so unnaturally to us that it first had to come to us as God in the flesh.

The love that can make marriage work between "I do" and death, in other words, is the love with which Christ loved us—a love that died for us while we yet sucked.

Marriage is a means of God's grace. God gets to us with his grace through the grace our beloved gives us. Forget what all the be-fruitful-and-multiply-family-values people vomit onto your TV screen, for my money this is the only Christian foundation to any formulation like Christian marriage. Like John the Baptist pointing his long, bony finger away from himself and onto Jesus, the forgiveness offered to you by your lover is a sacrament of that permanent forgiveness provided by Jesus's passion. And just as I say with bread and wine at the altar table every week, the promise of his passion is that it delivers us from captivity to our propensity to screw things up.

When Ali and I got married, I volunteered to file our taxes for our first joint return. I was still a graduate student. She was the one working to put me through school. Doing the taxes struck me as a fair and thoughtful division of labor. "It's just math, right?" I remember saying. Only, I also had a paying gig at a small church as a part-time pastor. Clergy taxes can be a conundrum, fine print no one walks you through in between New Testament

Greek and systematic theology. Confused, I put the tax returns away to do another day. It never came. Our insides are tricky. We're remarkably deft at deceiving ourselves. Whether I forgot to file them or avoided it altogether, I cannot say for sure. What I can vouch as the truth is that when Ali followed up and asked if I'd done them, I lied.

"Yep," I said reflexively.

And we said no more about it. Again, I can't say for sure, I thought no more about it. Until the following spring when the lie, like the interest owed, seemed to have compounded tenfold. Too big a lie to confront, I simply repeated it. I shelved the 1040 behind some old bills. When she asked again if I'd filed it, I said, "Sure."

Still skeptical about that word, *sin*? Sure, "the devil made me do it" can sound like a crappy excuse. *Captivity* can also be the best explanation.

Consider this. Even though I was determined to tell her the truth, I lied to her. And I kept on lying to her. *I don't want her to think I'm a liar who can't be trusted (that could hurt our relationship), so I'll just lie to her about it*, I thought to myself while ordering a Frosty at the Wendy's across from our apartment. I legitimately thought that sounded like a rational course of action.

Back when I was kid, during the bad old days, my dad had perpetrated the very same pretense, leaving my mom holding an outstanding IOU from the IRS. She couldn't pay it. Her dad bailed her out. The federal government was the only onlooker who could've considered their marriage a joint venture at that point. Ali and I were a year into our marriage when I discovered I'd become the man I'd begrudged all my growing up years. As a pastor, I hear church folks gossip all the time about the apple that fails to fall far away from the tree. What pewsitters don't realize maybe is that the apple, who is able to gauge its proximity to the tree whence it came, is able—eventually—to forgive its provenance.

Like that yarn about getting tangled up in the deceptions we weave, I kept the lie about having paid our taxes going for the first several years of marriage. Eventually, the truth of it became too big not to leak out all over our marriage. I never knew what couples meant when they said they had work to do in their relationship. I understood the day Ali found me out. The tears in her eyes confirmed she'd spied the treason in my own, confirming for me that I owed more than just back-taxes plus interest. I'd committed penalties against more than the IRS. Rightly, every spring thence sparked a rehearsal of the betrayal. In the months in between, anything that hinted at even a little white lie conjured up the bigger one between us.

On the outside we were fine. And after a while, we really were fine again. But on the inside, I loathed myself. I don't know about my cholesterol, but whenever I ventured too far inside, I struck up against shame in no time.

After I got stage-serious cancer, I went on medical leave for a long while. I volunteered to do our taxes that spring, and I discovered that I'd accidentally underpaid on the gifts we'd received to help with my gargantuan medical bills. I shit a brick. Instantly I feared this would be the keystone that brought our whole marriage down. It symbolized too much cumulative baggage between us. This was too severe a case of Post Tax Stress Disorder for us to survive. It sounds hyperbolic, but I'm not exaggerating when I say that I sweated telling her about the tax bill more than I did telling her about my cancer. The doctor had promised I didn't do anything to get the cancer; tumors, at least, weren't my fault.

I met her outside in the driveway when she came home. I told her. She asked how much. I told her. She nodded.

"It's okay," she said, "Thanks for telling me." As far as pregnant pauses go, this one felt like it had the gestation period of a manatee. "I forgive you," she said.

Not until I heard her say it did I feel freed to reply. "I'm sorry,"

I said, noting even then how her forgiveness preceded my repentance and most likely made it possible.

Nothing convinces you more that you bring nothing to the table like a lifetime of sitting at supper across from your spouse and seeing yourself as she sees you.

Yet, I'm loved.

Ali sees all the ways I'm still no different from that first "I do." Still she says "I do" every day. Seeing that she loves me all the same, I see her in a whole new light.

"I can't believe you keep saying 'I do' to me," I tell her from across the pillows more times than I care to count. It's neither a line for a love ballad nor for a "November Rain" video, but it's true nonetheless. Ali's the tonic against all the bullshit that comes naturally to a captive like me. She inoculates me against slippery self-flattery. She sees me as I am. Like God, she sees how much I still am as I've been. She grants to me a goodness that her life with me amply shows is not there. Were I to go spelunking inside me, nothing I found would corroborate what she's willing to reckon unto me.

She's grace. And thanks to her, or thanks to God *through* her, I'm something less than free but I'm a lot more than the opposite I was before.

When it comes to faithfulness in marriage, we tend to think not fooling around is the baseline definition. Sure, for someone who flirts with the girl in front of the fish monger's freezer, not fooling around is not a bad place to begin. Even more so, though, faithfulness means clinging to the promise inherent in her undeserved regard. Like a drowning man I hold on to the news that I am not what I do. I am not what I have done. Just as good, I am not what I will surely do despite my best efforts to do otherwise.

I am what she says I am. I am forgiven. And I am loved.

And if I am what my beloved says, then maybe I can trust that I am what the Beloved says too.

Learning how to make love again after a year of chemo-induced impotence is an awkward and hard (wink, wink) venture. After another night of finishing before we were done, I reiterated, "I can't believe you don't trade me in. Go ahead, I'll be fine. I'll find comfort in the arms of an elderly well-off widow."

"You're an idiot," she said and, I think, smiled in the dark.

"Hold me," I asked. I pled.

"I love you," she whispered.

I tell it to engaged couples all the time. What you're doing by saying "I do" is bestowing upon another person the power to do incredible damage to you with no other weapon than their words. My beloved's words have the power to kill me with their candor. But her words can also make me alive again with their gratuity. God's words of grace on a lover's lips can bridge the distance that can creep into any marriage bed. Indeed, a lover's grace is the closet analogy we have to how God in Christ closes the distance between heaven and earth. God's words of grace and forgiveness collapse time, in other words.

Speaking of time travel, now is as good a time as any to note how I have thus far neglected to sketch a picture of Ali for your mind's eye. She's a dead-ringer for Madeleine Stowe, Bruce Willis's costar in the science-fiction film *12 Monkeys*. She's got the same thick brunette hair, high cheekbones, serious eyes, shy smile, and strong, sexy shoulders. Back when Madeleine Stowe had a marquee Hollywood career, Ali used to get "You know who you look like?" from all sorts of strangers. It's a fitting likeness considering how in *12 Monkeys*, Bruce Willis is a survivor of an apocalypse. In the movie, he's thrust into a new, better time but still fated to die a too-soon death. Through the tragedy of time travel, the same disaster he's escaped only lurks waiting for him in his future. He's needy and confused and overwhelmed by his new situation. Even though he's a bad bet to invest your hopes in (and may even be a scoundrel), she sticks with him to the bitter end. She does so simply because that's who she is. He's bound in a cage he cannot see, but she loves him all the same. She loves him, chains and all.

To make it plain: Ali is more the preacher than me. I only preach a couple of hours on Sundays. Every day she proclaims to me the promise of a permanent pardon.

CHAPTER 4.

THE G-SPOT

So there is only one faith and one God—the one who makes promises.

—Martin Luther

To be or . . . line!

—Billy Crystal

MAKING LOVE A VERB

The memories stalked my mind.

Even in health, as my hair and strength returned after a year of chemo, I thought of my uncle Jim. Before I got sick, I looked like him. Same dark hair and thick brows and build. Same wry smile and jovial eyes and biceps. Sick, I had looked like Uncle Jim looked when he was sick. Over the course of a few years, leukemia sapped Jim's humor. The remedies squeezed every ounce of strength out of him. One last-ditch treatment after another dashed his family's hopes. Like me, Jim had two young kids and a wife, Cindy.

I knew it as a kid even before I knew it firsthand: the stress posed by his sickness onto everyone in his orbit was severe. His extended treatments and unpredictable recoveries, all of which occurred away in the hospital, were experienced by his family like military deployments. As happens to overseas soldiers, my uncle Jim became like a rumor to me. Worse, he faded into hazy memories for his kids.

His wife started seeing the grief counselor at the hospital.

Soon, she was *seeing* the hospital grief counselor.

Like I said, death can make you hopeless or horny or both. The baggage brought by his sickness was too much for her to bear. To call him a cuckold casts the blame on her. Likely, the leukemia is responsible. My dad had been the one to tell him the truth. He waited to tell him. He bided the time looking for a "good time" to break the news of his having been betrayed by the one for whom he was living and hoping the news wouldn't kill him. Whether it did, or the leukemia finally did, the doctors couldn't say. Uncle Jim got served divorce papers while lying in the hospital. He died not long after.

With every hiccup in my maintenance treatment, every real or perceived recurrence or relapse, the memory of Uncle Jim loomed over me like Jacob Marley. I knew, of course, that Ali would never forsake me. But then, I'm sure Jim would've said the same about Cindy before his sickness tore them asunder and left him alone to die. And I'm just as sure that Aunt Cindy would've crossed her fingers and hoped to die, sworn that she'd stick with him, stick a needle in her eye, until they were both parted by death. I was terrified of dying like Jim died. The memory of his marriage stalked me. I was fearful I'd end up crushed and cuckolded and calloused by losing my biggest reason to keep going. I still am afraid. I'd be an idiot not to be scared witless.

The point at which you most need to receive again the no-matter-what unconditionality of a promise is also the point at which the promise keeper is most apt to flee. Ironically, just like the double bind of a time-travel flick, the fear of the other fleeing is exactly what can produce the cloying conditions that provoke their flight.

Instead of *12 Monkeys*, I could've told you that Ali looks like Madeleine Stowe, who costarred in *The Last of the Mohicans*.

You're more likely to have seen the latter, but that would make me not the bald, frightened Bruce Willis but Daniel Day Lewis, the hatchet-throwing hero whose ripped chest heaves when he promises the damsel: "You're strong! You survive! You stay alive, no matter what occurs! I will find you! No matter how long it takes, no matter how far. I will find you!" Truth is, cancer reversed the casting. In the crucible of chemo and even after it, I was the dude in distress. I didn't feel like anyone's idea of a leading man.

Cancer left me feeling emasculated and insecure. And it showed. Or rather, it was audible.

Right after I came off medical leave and came back to work, I officiated a wedding of a young man in my congregation, Jake, whom I had known since he was a tween. I told myself knowing him so well demanded that I deviate from my standard wedding sermon. For some reason (I blame residual chemo brain), I thought it would be a smart rhetorical strategy to lead with a loaded question. I assumed the air of an authority rather than a perpetual understudy, and I posed it to them: "Here's a question: If love is a feeling, how can you possibly promise that to another? *Forever*!? You can't promise to feel a certain feeling every day for the rest of your life. If love is a feeling, how can you possibly promise another it will last?"

The bridesmaids' mouths dropped open. The bridal bouquet in her maid of honor's hands drooped limp. The sudden tension in the pews reminded me of the few times I'd mentioned politics from the pulpit. Attempting to sound provocative, I'd come across as pissy. I knew it. Still, I'm a manuscript preacher so I stuck stubbornly to my script:

> If love is a feeling, then is it any wonder the odds are better than even that it won't last? The poet in Ecclesiastes who tells us that "two are better than one" also tells us a chapter earlier about the fleetingness of our feelings. "There comes a time for every matter under heaven," the poet writes, "a time to be born and a time to die. A time to embrace and a time to refrain from embracing. A time to

keep silent. A time to speak. A time to laugh. A time to weep. A time to mourn, and a time to love. God has made everything suitable for a given time," the poet writes. But again, there's the question: If love is just a feeling how can the poet of Ecclesiastes describe it like that? If love is just a feeling how can God assign a time to it? Of all the things in our lives, our feelings are the part of us we have the least control over. You can't promise to feel a certain feeling every day for the rest of your life.

When you turn away from Ecclesiastes and into the New Testament, love isn't just something you promise to another. It's something you're commanded to give another. When a rich lawyer asks Jesus for the key to it all, Jesus says: "Love the Lord completely and love your neighbor as yourself." The night before he dies, when Jesus washes his friends' feet, he tells them: "I give you a new commandment: love one another just as I have loved you." And when the apostle Paul writes to the Colossians, just before he commands husbands and wives to love one another, Paul commands them to "bear with each other, to forgive one another, to put on love." Those are all imperatives. They're commands. Demands. They're obligations. Here's the thing.

I held it for a moment and looked around the sanctuary.

You can't force a feeling. You can't command an emotion. You can only command an action. In Scripture, love is an action first and a feeling second. Jesus and Paul take a word we use as a noun, *love*, and they make it a verb, which is the exact opposite of how the culture has taught us all to think about love. We think of love as a noun, as a feeling, as something that happens to us, which means then we think we must feel love in order to give it. But [I warned like I was wiser than I am], that's a recipe for a broken relationship.

Because when you think you must feel love first in order to give it, then when you don't feel love toward the other you stop offering them love. Sure, it's a feeling that sparks a relationship, but the condition for an enduring relationship, the condition for a relationship that can last a lifetime, is making love a verb.

Even if I'm only inchoately aware of it, I know the primary person I have in mind when I preach is myself. I'm most often the one who needs to hear the sermons I deliver. In this case, my intended audience was the frightened version of myself. I was preaching to the me who worried that Ali needed to hear it. Not only did I crib generously from C. S. Lewis, I projected my anxiety on to Jake and his bride, Martha. Through them, I passively tried to persuade Ali, seated seven rows back, to practice what I preach. Fearing the unconditionality of Ali's promise to me was down to the last dregs, I opted to emphasize its obligations.

The week before the wedding I'd gone to the infusion center for maintenance chemo. It had triggered tremors in my body, a muted version of the reaction I had experienced to my very first urgent dosage over a year earlier. Back then my oncologist had explained the chemo caused tremors as it broke up the bulky tumors that covered all over my insides. This time the doc had attempted to reassure it away by telling me that the tremors were probably caused by an allergic reaction. The sword of Damocles that had been hung up safely on our wall was again looming over our marriage.

When I told Ali about the tremors, she didn't cry. I'd expected her to cry. I wished she'd cried. Instead she asked questions, questions I couldn't answer. Asking, she looked exhausted. Spent. Looking at the photos from Jake's wedding, the camera didn't lie. I looked anxious and insecure. The Dixie Chicks song the bride and groom played at their party captured it better than I could admit. Afraid I was sick again, I was terrified that she was ready to run.

The day before Jake and Martha said "I do," the doctor had done a scan just to make sure. I was still adrift in the limbo of three-to-five business days, waiting for the results. I was scared shitless. So I decided to *should* all over the bride and groom:

> The condition for an enduring relationship, the condition for a relationship that can last a lifetime, is making love a verb. That's how Jesus can command us to love our enemies. Jesus can't force us to feel a certain way about our enemies, but Jesus can command us to do concrete loving actions for our enemies knowing that those loving acts might eventually transform how we feel.

Paul says: "Clothe yourselves with compassion, kindness, humility, gentleness and patience so that the peace of Christ may rule in your hearts." In other words, where you invest loving actions, loving feelings will follow. You should do love, then you will feel it, in that order.

In your marriage you may not feel gentle, but you should act gentle. You may not feel compassionate on a given day, but just as you would a child, you should listen and show them compassion. You may not feel patient and kind tomorrow night, but tomorrow evening what you should do is muster up some patience and kindness.

You can't promise each other the feeling of love that's not the covenant you make today. The condition of your covenant is that if you are married, then you will do the doing of love even in the absence of love's feelings.

I actually used the word *condition*.

There's a reason grooms and brides get a bystander in a robe and a collar to broker their nuptials. An unconditional promise of forever requires either a straitjacket or blind faith.

Conditional promises strike us as reasonable. An unconditional promise, however, makes no sense to us at all. It strikes us as reckless. Where a conditional promise can come couched in terms of advice and obligation, an unconditional promise can only be given and received in terms of trust.

Fearing that death was doing its work to part us, trust was my problem.

The monthly upkeep chemo was meant to maintain not only my life but my marriage. Through no fault of Ali's, I feared our marriage had a reached a fragile point. I worried we were near to getting to the thicket of fine print attached to the contract we'd signed to one another. If it hadn't been before, our latest scare over a recurrence of cancer made it unavoidably clear. A promise without condition *to me* seemed to commit *her* to too much downside. It required too much trust to think that she could or, really, *should* stick with me through the underside of our unconditional promise.

It may sound like a hypocritical confession coming from a professional confessor, but it took too much faith to believe in the unconditional promise.

BALLS TO THE WALL

Every good preacher knows it. You shouldn't preach about a wound that's still fresh or festering. You can't proclaim the gospel when grief or grievance get in the way. I had no business preaching about marriage when I was terrifically anxious about my own.

My listeners loved it.

With a magician's sleight of hand, I'd twisted their balls-to-the-wall, no-matter-what "I do's" into the if/then lingo of conditionality. And I disguised it all as good advice. I suspect that's why, in the end, the sermon killed. We're all born lawyers. We like conditions. Like the Israelites when offered the golden calf as an alternative to the real thing, Jake and Martha's well-wishers ate it up. Once they got past the provocation of my initial questions, the sermon "preached." Judging from the feedback, it struck all the married folk in the room as sound counsel. It seemed to the singles, who were brave enough to broach it with me, as countercultural. They heard it as a corrective to the subjective, overly romanticized notions of love we imbibe by the cultural ether. Perhaps on the cultural score, it was a true word. But as far as advice goes, at least in the incomplete terms in which I'd cast it, it was worse than bad advice.

It was a lie.

Ask any woman who's ever felt the obligation to put out if, having done so, it left her happy, horny, and hungry for more. Hardly, I'll bet. Giving out acts of love even when you do not feel love (though it might please your partner) will not produce in you feelings of love.

As it is with head, so it is with our hearts.

Doing your *Christian* duty, in marriage or in any other

relationship, does not determine correlative desire. Acting forgiving toward your spouse even though you do not *feel* forgiving may make your spouse feel pardoned. But it will not produce in you feelings of forgiveness. Even listening to your spouse when you do not feel like listening may grease the relationship wheels. Yet it will not produce in you genuine empathy; in fact, it will nurture the opposite in you. My wedding sermon was neither good advice nor good exegesis of Scripture. It was a recipe for resentment and bitterness. Exhort a bride or groom to be forgiving (because they ought to be forgiving) and, sure enough, it will lead to them begrudging one another. Or, they'll begrudge the God from whom such burdens flow.

In either its noun or verb forms, *love* as demand does not determine a loving desire in you. Putting out any sort of love simply because it's your Christian *duty* is likelier to leave you impatient and unkind and cold. Love performed according to if/then conditions will leave you likelier to leave your lover. Yet, in my fear of being left, I laid the oughts on Ali. I just couldn't muster the faith to believe that when she'd said "I do" to me, she ever anticipated that one day I'd become my uncle.

Having become Jim, I was afraid Ali would cry uncle.

The promises we make one another die in their conditionality. At their wedding, I framed Jake and Martha's promises in terms of if/then conditions because, even if subconsciously, I feared death made marriage no different than any other of our relationships. All our promises end with a silent, unspoken addendum: *If I live long enough.* All the other so-called promises we make in life are conditional. They pose the future as a demand or an obligation. *Because you're my boss, I will be respectful toward you. If you burn me, then I will retaliate. I'll be your friend so long as I can trust you. If you love me, I'll love you back.* Such "promises" bind the future to the past in that the promised future is contingent upon fulfilling prior conditions.

By contrast, the unconditional promise given by bride and

groom poses the future not as a demand, command, or obligation. An unconditional promise instead offers the future as sheer gift no matter what (sickness or health) precedes it. Whereas conditional promises make the future depend upon the past, unconditional promises make the past depend upon the future. An unconditional promise allows its recipient to appropriate the past and reframe it in light of the promise because the future does not depend on it. Rather, the past now depends on the promised future. Thus: *I know I've been impatient and unkind but neither my impatience nor my unkindness can separate me from the one who loves me without condition.*

The unconditional promise of marriage is that you are accepted and loved in spite of who you have been or what you have done. Therefore, the promise of marriage is that you will love your beloved regardless of who they are or what they do or what happens to the two of you through nobody's fault but your blood chemistry. The promise of marriage, which can be received by trust alone, is that you will be loved by your beloved no matter the shitty hand life deals the two of you.

To paraphrase Martin Luther:

> The conditional promise says "Do this and you will be loved, but it is never done." The unconditional promise says "You are loved always and forever no matter what you do or do not do. So, relax and get on with your life together."

Counterintuitively, only the latter, says Scripture, only the unconditional promise has the power to inspire in us the love that the oughts exhort.

I had put it exactly backward to Jake and Martha. Loving feelings do not come by putting out. Loving feelings come by receiving love. Specifically, love comes by receiving and revisiting the promise that your future together is not determined by your present. No matter how impatient or unkind you are, you are loved.

The promise produces love.

Feelings of love do not follow by obeying the conditions of a contract. Feelings of love come from hearing again the unconditionality of your lover's promised love.

Here's what you realize when you're staring at your DOB on a clear bag of chemo wondering when its bookend date will come up on the calendar, and here's why I ended up *shoulding* all over Jake and Martha at their wedding: there is no refuge from time for any of us. We can neither guarantee our future nor offer it as a gift to another. It's not ours to give. The future doesn't belong to us. No matter how unconditional their no-matter-what promises to one another sound, the very time-bound bodies with which bride and groom pledge their vows betray the stubborn conditionality of their pledge. A no-matter-what, come-what-may unconditional promise requires the one gift husband and wife cannot give one another: a future unbounded by death.

Death makes all our promises conditional.

That's a lesson I learned at another wedding.

TRANS-GENTILE

My mom and I were talking politics. I had the phone cradled against my shoulder, stirring a roux for dinner that was nearly as dark as my mom's mood. Ali was helping our son, Gabriel, with his math homework.

"Maybe I will move to Canada," my mom said and sighed.

"Canada! They eat ketchup flavored Doritos in Canada—how is that a thing?! And Canada is responsible for Céline Dion and Nickelback. Think about that, Mom: Justin Bieber and Tom Ford don't even crack the Top Ten of Canadiens for whom Canada should have to issue a global apology. Though, Canada did give the world that babe who played Kim in *24*."

"She's beautiful."

"Yes, she is . . ." I said and immediately my mind wandered to the film in which she costarred with Emile Hirsch, *The Girl Next Door*.

Ali rolled her eyes at me and said, "Oh, brother."

"Jason? Jason are you still there?"

"Huh? Yeah, I'm still here. I was just . . . thinking. Look, forget this Canada nonsense. Mom, you hate the snow, and no matter how much I begged you as a kid you never let me grow a mullet."

"I hate mullets."

"See, forget Canada. I'll tell you, though, if I had a Jew in my family tree I'd move to Israel, at least their president is actually a conservative."

"But my grandparents were Jewish."

"But *what*?!"

"My grandparents, they were both Jewish."

"But . . . but . . . but . . . that means my great-grandparents were *Jewish*."

"Uh, huh" my mother said blankly, clearly not registering that this was a seismic revelation for someone like me who, let's just say, is salaried and pensioned *not* to be Jewish.

"But . . . but . . . but . . . *that means I'm Jewish*," I whispered while turning down the volume on my iPhone.

"Yeah, I guess it does."

No joke, my next thoughts, in rapid-fire succession:

1. Holy bleep, how have I not heard about this before?!

2. No wonder I'm so funny.

3. Thank God I'm already circumcised.

4. I could spin this into a book! Christian clergyman discovers his previously unknown Jewish identity. It practically writes itself.

As for the screen, it'd be the perfect follow up to *La La Land* for Ryan Gosling.

As soon as I got off the phone with my mom, I pitched the book idea to my editor. I'd even come up with some snappy titles such as: *Riddler on the Roots, Goy Meets God,* and, my personal favorite, *Trans-Gentile.*

Nevertheless, my editor replied that until I actually convert and move myself and my family to the promised land, what I had was a good idea for a blogpost. Not a book. Of course, that same editor came up with a terrible book title like *Cancer Is Funny,* so I figured what the hell does he know.

Ali couldn't resist when I told her:

"Funny, you've always acted as though you're God's gift to the world. Now, it turns out, you really are—you're chosen!"

I've got to find out more about what this means! I thought.

In the weeks and months that followed, I studied up. I researched the State of Israel's Right of Return rules. I qualify. I tested my DNA through ancestry.com, the results of which bore out what my mother had told me, that I am of Jewish lineage by way of Austria. And thanks to Genghis Khan raping and pillaging his way across Europe, I also have some Mongolian in me too, a Patton Oswalt joke that turned out to be true.

DNA in hand, I consulted with a rabbi about what books he recommends to potential converts. At his advice I read the Tanakh, *Living a Jewish Life* by Anita Diamant, *Judaism's Ten Best Ideas* by Arthur Green, and *To Life: A Celebration of Jewish Being and Thinking* by Harold Kushner. And, because Judaism is a religion that developed out of its celebrations, he suggested I also read *The Jewish Way: Living the Holidays* by Irving Greenberg.

No longer a goy, I wasn't coy about using an interfaith wedding on my calendar as a learning opportunity.

I hadn't met the rabbi with whom I was officiating. I just had a name, and he only had mine, so the day of the rehearsal I waited for him at the bar outside the Hilton ballroom where the wedding would be the next day, vaguely aware that I'd just cast myself in one of those hackneyed jokes.

So a rabbi and a minister walk into a bar . . .

The groom in the wedding was nominally Christian, and his

parents wanted a pastor to participate in the ceremony so that *their* parents would be satisfied. I didn't know anyone in the wedding. And that made me nervous.

I'd presided at a couple of other interfaith weddings before, and I'd always found them to be clumsy affairs. Rather than bringing together the best of two religious traditions, which is always the misguided fantasy the bride and groom have in their minds, they more often turn into an awkward clergy duel where the liturgy feels like it's been cut-and-pasted together by a committee of pushy, future in-laws needing to justify themselves.

Given my previous experiences, it made me uneasy that I'd never met this rabbi. It made me even more nervous that the bride had told me on several occasions that the rabbi had no interest in meeting with me or even talking on the phone prior to the wedding rehearsal. All I could coax from him, through her, was an agreement to meet in the hotel lounge just before the rehearsal itself. I sat at the hotel bar waiting for a rabbi I'd never met, every now and then looking in the bar mirror to see if I could spot him behind me.

I did. He was easier to spot than I expected, like he'd just stepped out of a Woody Allen movie. He was old with curly white hair and with his disheveled, world-weary appearance looked not a little like Columbo. But what caught my eye was the yarmulke that was fastened crookedly on the back of his head: it had a navy and white New York Yankees insignia on it.

The rabbi had a harder time identifying me. Clearly expecting me to be older than I was, I watched him behind me in the mirror as he approached at least ten other people in the lounge, asking them in a thick German accent if they were "Rev. Michelle." He asked a woman who was sipping a martini and redoing her make-up. He asked an Asian businessman who was reading the *Wall Street Journal.* He even asked one of the black-suited bellhops before he decided to take a chance and ask me.

Once he found me, he introduced himself and then he sat

down at the bar next to me. And there we were: me with my Bible, him with his Tanakh, sitting in front of a Sam Adams tap. That's when he smiled and said loudly: "Gee, this is like one of those jokes where a rabbi and a priest walk into a bar."

"Actually it's even funnier than that . . ." and I proceed to tell him how I'd recently discovered that I too was a part of the chosen people. But he just furrowed his brows and assumed a distressed look on his face, like he was holding in a fart, and when I finished he coughed up a limp, "Ha ha." He'd thought I'd been telling him a joke, and not finding a punch line, he'd offered me a mercy chuckle.

"Don't get circumcised yet my friend," he said. "If you want to be one of us you'll have to learn to deliver a joke better than that."

The mustachioed bartender apparently didn't think either of us was funny. Plus, I can't imagine two clergy sitting at a bar is good for business.

We sat there for a while as he tried to decide how best to "accommodate" me in the ceremony. I waited as he stared over his order of worship until he finally said: "Well, why don't you just do the vows. It'll be hard for you to mess that up."

As we got up to go to the rehearsal, the rabbi asked the bartender if he could have a glass.

"What do you want in it?" the bartender asked.

"Nothing, I just want a glass," the rabbi replied.

"For the wedding," I explained to the bartender. "You know: mazel tov!"

I looked at the rabbi and shook my head in feigned disgust at the bartender's ignorance. "Gentiles," I said with a tsk-tsk tone of voice.

"Ha!" the rabbi laughed. "Maybe we'll do a bris after the wedding after all!"

The bartender did a double take and said: "Wait, you really are a rabbi? And you're . . ." he asked looking at me.

"Yes," I said. "I'm Reverend Michelle."

At the start of the wedding rehearsal, the groom's grand-mother, who, as far as I could tell was the only practicing Christ-ian there, complained that she couldn't hear. The rabbi suggested that since I was only responsible for the vows, I should go sit down next to the grandmother and repeat for her the meaning of the Jewish wedding rituals as he explained them to the wedding party.

So I sat down next to the old lady. She insisted on holding my hand for some reason, and first I watched the rabbi pull out a long, ornate scroll from a cardboard tube.

It was the *ketubah*, the Jewish wedding contract. It looks like an illuminated page from a medieval Bible. The signing of the *ketubah* begins the marriage ceremony. I listened as the rabbi explained to the groom that the *ketubah* obligates him to provide his new wife with food, clothing, and marital relations.

I heard the groomsmen onstage snigger to themselves when the rabbi said marital relations. Evidently the groom's grand-mother's hearing wasn't as bad as she alleged because, stroking my hand with her thumb, she said aloud, "I miss my Roger roger-ing me."

I coughed out my gum.

Anxious to change the subject, I continued interpreting for her, as the rabbi went on to instruct the groomsmen in how they should carry and hold the *chuppah*, the wedding canopy that sym-bolizes God's protection. I repeated to her the rabbi's explanation that the groom was supposed to cover his bride with a veil during the service and pray over her the words of Rebecca from Genesis: "May you, our sister, become thousands of myriads." I whispered into the grandmother's ear while the rabbi taught the bride how she was to step circles around her groom three times, symboliz-ing the three virtues of marriage from the prophet Hosea: right-eousness, justice, and loving kindness.

The rings and vows were to come just before the breaking of the glass. So after the rabbi finished explaining the symbolism of the three circles to the bride, I left the old lady in the wheelchair and walked up onstage, ready finally to do my part.

"Roger, where are you going?" she asked.

I stuck the program in the back pages of my prayer book as I found my place. Asking for their rings, I held them up as I had done at Jake and Martha's wedding and a hundred others like it.

"These rings," I explained to the wedding party, "are an outward and visible sign of God's inward, invisible, unconditional grace signifying the unconditional promise these two make to one another."

"No," the rabbi said next to me, as though we were haggling in an Arab market.

"Come again?" I asked.

"No" the rabbi said again.

"No what?"

"No, it's not an unconditional promise. Only God can make an unconditional promise."

"Is that so?" I said, irritated and thinking that even if I needed to be circumcised I wouldn't want it to be by him. He was upstaging me.

"The only promise that can be unconditional is a promise that has death behind it."

Without realizing it, the rabbi had made me a Jew for Jesus.

A PROMISE BACKED BY DEATH

The one gift required for us to pledge an unconditional promise is the one gift we cannot give: our futures. We could erase all our other obligations. Our time-bound bodies would still qualify every open-ended promise we dared ever to make. It's right there in the vows plainly put. I'd just never noticed it before the pushy rabbi pointed it out to me. Any promise of no-matter-what love stops short of unconditionality right at the nose of that "until death parts us."

Death makes every promise conditional.

But the rabbi with the Yankees yarmulke was only half right. An irreversible promise requires not just death to be behind it. Any unconditional promise also requires resurrection.

I suppose there's a reason that in the Gospels Jesus is constantly commanding his friends not to fear. When we're afraid, we're apt to put our faith not in him but in ourselves. Or worse, we'll put all our faith in our own ability to *have* faith. Frightened, we can forget that Jesus is not only the object of our faith, he's the subject and substance of our faith too. The exhortations I'd offered at Jake and Martha's wedding, which may have sounded like seasoned advice to some, really were invitations to them to place their trust in themselves. *If you just have faith in your own doing of love, then love will come*, I essentially told them.

In my own fear of being forsaken like my uncle before me, I had correctly fixed upon the enormity of our unconditional promise to one another. But I had forgotten that the faith required by our unconditional promise is not faith in our character. It is not faith in our power to uphold our pledge. The no-matter-what love of marriage requires faith from one another, yes. But it's not faith *in* one another; it's one another's faith in the truth and reality of their own baptisms.

The faith required by marriage is faith in baptism. Baptism is the outward, visible sign of the unconditional promise called the gospel. It's all right there in the wedding service. I'd just never noticed it until I feared my own marriage was stretched too taut to survive:

> I ask you now, in the presence of God and these people, to declare your intention to enter into union with each other through the grace of Jesus Christ, who calls you into union with himself as acknowledged in your baptism.

I'd given Jake and Martha advice to which Easter was only incidental. The wedding service, however, presumed that their promises to one another made no sense whatsoever if Jesus Christ, having died for their sins, had not been raised to newness of life and they with him by their baptisms.

Marriage does not require faith in one another. Marriage requires faith that whatever slights lay ahead of us, they're all already behind us. We can give our future to one another because, in our baptisms, we're already in the One who is without beginning or end. Baptism frees us to live (by faith) as though everything is in the past where all is forgiven and every account is settled. We can not only make an irreversible promise to one another, we can live up to it too.

Baptism makes marriage a covenant we can keep. We can give one another unconditional love because we are already grafted into the love that conquers all. We're safe in him. No matter how we slip up and make a mess of our marriage, it's all subsumed under the banner of the unconditional promise: "It is finished." Everything we do to another is forgivable because everything we do to one another has already been forgiven.

We can get through anything in marriage because everything has already been overcome.

I realize all of the above may sound like pie-in-the-sky Christian crazy. Certainly it's no guarantee of happily ever after. But for my money, apart from such faith, tying your life to another imperfect creature for the purposes of forever is insane.

At Jake's wedding, in my ill-fitting suit, my hair not quite grown back, I looked like the late version of Uncle Jim—he'd been a lawyer. After the ceremony, Ali and I took the boys to the wedding reception. It was a party, I'm sure, like the one Jesus graced at Cana. It was a party with music and couples and sons and daughters and grandchildren and childhood friends and dancing and candles flickering in the dusk. Kids played, and old men and old women watched while they held hands. Dirty plates were scattered on the tables. Wrinkled napkins wadded on top of them. Empty cocktail glasses and half-full bottles of wine sweating in the summer heat.

We sat at a table near the rear of the dance floor with the groom's parents. Jake's mom had been my son Gabriel's music teacher in preschool not too many years ago. She was still young and beautiful. A few months before the wedding, she'd suffered a massive stroke from which she was still recovering. She had difficulty getting around. Words and names still slipped her grasp. The stroke had locked her eyes in an unfocused, disconcerting, stare. Following conversation was just as hard for her. Despite everything he'd been through with me, I could tell her state left Gabriel uneasy. He looked at her uncomfortably and looked away from her when she spoke. But Gabriel watched intently, I noticed, as her husband patiently waited on her. Gabriel watched while he helped her with her food or in her chair. Gabriel watched as he kindly redirected her back to a conversation. He listened while her husband filled in the gaps for her with grace.

Jake's dad never once acted overwhelmed or annoyed or disappointed or sad.

As the party tapered off and some of the guests had gone, Jake's dad helped his wife up out of her chair. Setting her cane against the table, he all but carried her to the dance floor. In the center of the floor, while some cheesy country song played, he held his wife up against himself. He danced with her. She looked up at him. Her crooked eyes beamed. Then she rested her head against his shoulder. From a distance, to any unknowing stranger, they would've looked like a high-school homecoming king and queen.

Ali and I sat at our table and wept.

"It must be hard for him," Gabriel said.

"I'm sure it's hard for them both," Ali said. "But they love each other so it's okay."

"I don't know what I'd do if I found out I had to do all of that for my wife," our older son, Alexander, admitted.

"No one is ever ready for what happens in marriage," Ali

answered. "Marriage makes you ready for what happens in marriage."

"Still, I bet it's really hard for him."

"I'm sure it's hard," Ali said. "But when you know the other person loves you unconditionally, no matter what, you don't think about what you have to do. You just actually want to do it."

If you trust it, marriage is a gospel promise with your name on it. The truth is, everyone who dares to say "I do" is a damsel in distress, hoping that no matter where life takes them Jesus will be their Daniel Day Lewis. His love will find you.

Ali leaned over and, over the top of Gabriel's head, she kissed my cheek. Then, though she hates dancing, she stood up. She grabbed my hand. She pulled me to her just as the DJ began to play the Dolly Parton song, made famous by Whitney Houston's *Bodyguard* cover, "I Will Always Love You."

Tears still in her eyes, she smiled at me. And then whispered into my ear a sweet nothing. I smiled, thinking the fundamentalists might be onto something when they forbid dancing. Maybe they're right to suspect dancing will lead to lovemaking, for in this instance, they were right.

CHAPTER 5.

SMOKIN' HOT

Adam said to Eve: "Stand back. We don't know how big it gets."
       —*Prairie Home Companion*, Audience Submission

Do not deprive one another . . .
       —1 Corinthians 7

A BEGGAR FOR BLEEDING CHARITY

The song playing at Jake's wedding took me back twenty odd years to when my mother first uttered those words that have since gone on to become synonymous with American exceptionalism: "Let's go to Costco." We'd never been before, and if my mom was prepared for what we found inside, I sure wasn't. It was like a shopping mall for the apocalypse.

"No wonder all my Mormon friends' parents shop here."

In addition to a tub of frozen pork BBQ and a gallon of black olives, that day I talked my mom into buying me a copy of the Stephen King novel *Gerald's Game,* a book that in hindsight should've been titled *69 Shades of Grey* and should never have been allowed into the hands or the mind of fifteen-year-old me. My mom bought herself a compact disk. It was the soundtrack to the major motion picture *The Bodyguard.*

In case you don't remember, *The Bodyguard* was the nineties version of the *Twilight* movies, except instead of werewolves and vampires it starred a balding, swollen Kevin Costner as the hero and Whitney Houston as a pop star whose troubled personal life echoed Houston's own. The movie was typical for both stars. Whitney Houston sang as she always did on stage, and Kevin Costner attempted to act as he always does on screen.

Giddy with romantic projection, my mom laid the CD into the shopping cart and headed to the register. As you no doubt remember, *The Bodyguard* lasted longer in the daydreams of suburban women than it did at the box office, but the theme song from the film became a sensation. It sold a million albums in its first week. It won a Grammy. In the two decades since, it's sold forty-five million copies, and, according to Wikipedia, it remains the bestselling movie soundtrack of all time.

When we got to my mother's Honda Accord, she frantically ripped the CD from its packaging with her teeth, like a solider trying to staunch a platoon mate's bleeding. She turned the key in the ignition, slid the CD into the mouth of the console, and then, like a desert wanderer reaching out toward a mirage that's too good to be true, she pressed the play button: "I Will Always Love You." After a few moments, she pressed pause and looked over at me and in complete seriousness said: "Isn't this great? Kevin Costner's just so . . ." We sat there in the car, in the parking lot, in the afternoon rain, listening to the next three tracks of *The Bodyguard* soundtrack and then "I Will Always Love You" three more times.

I'm enough of a Dolly Parton fan to have been the only straight dude at her show in town last spring (which also made me the only dude not wearing a pink cowboy hat), but, to my mind, between Whitney's cover and Dolly's original there's no contest. In this case at least, Billboard doesn't lie. What gives Whitney Houston's rendition the greater depth and resonance is the story in which it is found—or rather, the power of Whitney's song from *The Bodyguard* is the presence in the story of a bodyguard;

that is, one who is willing to die for her, in her place, as her substitute.

"I will always love you" is a shallow lie. Or, worse, it's a dangerous self-deception unless it is first not a declaration but a response. "I will always love you" is only true or possible at all if generated by a prior and greater love. Those who dare to say "I do" to one another do not assume they have a greater ability to do love than those who cross their fingers or settle for lesser promises. On the contrary, to say "I do" to an unconditional promise, to give another what only God can give, is to acknowledge that if the promise is to hold together at all (still a big IF) then it will only be by God's own active agency in the marriage.

There's a reason that Christian husbands and wives exchange their vows under the name of Father, Son, and Holy Spirit. They're admitting that, no matter what the love songs say, their relationship is not exceptional. It requires more than the two of them. The two of them do not bring to their relationship any attributes that make them more likely than any other couple to live out their conditionless promise. If they will prove to love one another always, then it will be because God has been found to be with them. Every pairing of bride and groom by promise is problematic.

Every marriage needs a miracle.

God reveals himself most fully and perfectly in the crucified Jesus Christ. It's foolish for us to suppose then that God will be present to us in marriage in ways that are any less expected. Every marriage needs a miracle. But the particular manner in which the miracle of God's presence comes to us is one from which we'd rather absent ourselves. The God of Jesus Christ never ceases to be the God of the cross.

In marriage as in life, God meets us particularly on the horizon of our suffering and shame. God shows himself in our pain and rejection. God reveals himself alongside our humiliation, our weakness, and our stark-naked vulnerability. Who would say "I do" if they knew ahead of time that their marriage committed them to meeting God in the cross? Who would go through with their vows if they knew those vows invited them to come and die?

To make another your beloved, and for it to have any hope of the "always" of which Whitney sang, is to be willing to be made a beggar in need of the bleeding charity of God. Anyone who says "I do" to a no-matter-what promise needs God to create in them the possibility of such unconditional love.

Therein lies the rub. The way God creates love in us is the same way God created all that is around us: from nothing. In other words, in order to say "I do"—and for that "I do" to amount to something—you must be willing for God to reduce you to nothing. The only way from if/then conditions to unconditional love goes through the cross.

SAD FUCKING

"Alexa, play Christopher Cross," our friend Hannah ordered in the direction of her kitchen counter. We'd been listening to Alexa play Cross's song "Arthur's Theme" on repeat a few times. It had sparked a nostalgic debate between Hannah, her husband Ryan, and me about the merits of '80s yacht rock. Ali, the only one of the four of us to have had a healthy, happy childhood, did not share our zeal for the genre. "My mom actually listened to good music when we were kids," Ali explained.

"Yeah, that's because she loved you. Go screw yourself!" Ryan said through his big Jersey grin and then smacked her across the shoulder to make sure she was enjoying his humor as much as he was.

Alexa finally obliged after having first started to play "Jump" by Kris Kross. Christopher Cross's classic single "Ride like the Wind" came on loud, and Hannah wiped her suddenly moist eyes. "Some nights it was all I could do. I'd pour some wine and play shitty yacht rock just to take my mind off how my marriage was falling apart and there wasn't anything I could about it."

They'd invited Ali and me over for dinner. Our kids were playing in the TV room. Empty bowls of gumbo streaked with oil and scallions were pushed into the center of the table against the lit candles. Hannah and I had started to sing "Arthur's Theme" like you do when you're on your second or third glass of wine. Ryan had been telling us about pitching his book to producers in Hollywood: "They want to turn it into another *Dead Man Walking* social-justice movie. How many more white-lawyer-saves-black-con movies do we need? But, hey, if it makes some money . . ."

"You ought to pitch it as a story about your marriage instead," I told him. "Put the case and Wayne's pardon in the background and move the two of you to the foreground. Make it so it's a death-row story where your marriage is the prison."

"Holy shit that could work. It definitely was true," Ryan said, looking at Hannah, who looked grateful and in love. "During the case, for years, I'd be down in freaking death row, on the free side of the plexiglass, but half the time—because of us," he pointed across the table at Hannah, "I felt like the one who was doing time."

Ryan proved to be one of my best friends when I first got sick. He was there to catch me when I passed out in chemo, and I was there to reciprocate by holding his hand when he got his vasectomy. A white-collar criminal defense attorney, Ryan got recruited by his law firm a few years to work on a pro bono capital case in Texas. Ryan's the kind of lawyer you imagine is a good lawyer because in a different life or under different circumstances, he'd be doing time for a long con.

Wayne had been convicted of a cop killing after a check-cashing heist in Houston had gone wrong. Despite an alibi that never changed, an absence of any DNA evidence, and an IQ of 67, qualifying him as mentally handicapped, Wayne had been sentenced to death by the State of Texas. A former public defender,

Ryan says his BS radar is fine-tuned enough to ferret out liars, and after he met Wayne for the first time in the penitentiary, he threw up in the prison parking lot. "I knew in my bones that Wayne was innocent and that he was probably going to die because I couldn't save his life," Ryan once told me. "I felt completely helpless and totally responsible."

The case consumed him for nearly a decade, pulling him away from his wife and kids for months at a time. His faith frayed. His other work suffered, and his marriage almost fell apart. Had he not happened upon exculpatory evidence that the prosecution had been hiding all along, Wayne would've died.

"I love Wayne, but I hated that Ryan had taken his case. All I could think about was that if Wayne died, the man I married would die too," Hannah said. "I just lived stuck in this constant dread for a decade that Wayne would be executed and I'd be left living with a man who was dead on the inside for the rest of our life together."

"I was burnt out and terrified," Ryan said, "and I'd come home and she'd be depressed and irritable. Then I'd get pissed because I just wanted peace and quiet and to get some. It sounds messed up, but there were months between us where I actually preferred to be with Wayne on death row. I'd go to prison to escape my wife. Wayne at least was grateful for whatever version of me showed up."

"Each time he was home, we'd start to have sad sex, and I'd lie there wondering if there'd be less of him than last time," Hannah said sipping wine.

"And, J knows, I can't afford to lose any of me in that department," Ryan laughed and whispered to Ali.

"There's your title for your pilot," I said, "call it 'Sad Fucking.'"

Hannah laughed. Ryan didn't. But he smiled.

"It *was*," Ryan said. "Here I was doing 'God's work' on death row and my marriage was hell. Hannah and I—we were down to nothing. I guess God was too busy in the prison to help me out at home, huh?"

"Is that a pastor question?" I asked. He didn't answer. He was waiting for me to answer. "If God was busy anywhere, I think God was just as busy in your 'nothing,'" I said.

"Think so?" Ryan asked like a wise ass.

I nodded but then qualified it with a shrug of the shoulders: "Nothing is what God needs to do anything."

"Maybe that's why we didn't get *through* it until we were both able to own how we were stuck *in* it, together" Hannah added.

"And you weren't alone. God's present in every prison," I said, "not just the ones with cement blocks and iron bars. Thus endeth the sermon."

"Well, we're free at last, baby," Ryan raised his Coke Zero and tipped it toward Hannah who beamed. "Here's to no more sad fucking. Although, let's be honest, I'm still pretty sad in the sack."

"You don't have much to work with," I joked.

"But the little I have is all hers."

"I don't think I can take it one more day," Christopher Cross crooned. His song "Say You'll Be Mine" had started to play.

"It's a miracle we made it," Hannah said across the candlelight. Judging from her smile, she didn't realize it was true.

"Alexa play 'Ride like the Wind,'" she said toward the kitchen sink and started to sing along when it came on.

"You really think I should pitch it as a story about our marriage?"

I nodded.

"Our story's so particular," Ryan said. "Innocent man on death row, marriage with a noose tied around it? You think people could relate to a story like ours?"

"Yes," Ali said a little too quickly. And then she brushed her finger across mine.

A PLEASURE TO MAKE YOUR REACQUAINTANCE

I gave her a hickey by mistake the first time.[1]

Our bodies and mouths and hands and hips moved too fast and urgent. We were too hungry. It was like we were teens again. We were acting on instinct and the advice of adolescent rumors alone. I tried too hard. And I tried too hard to stay hard. It's odd, we coo at babies and smile at the pregnant bellies before them, but we regard hickeys almost as tramp stamps. We act embarrassed at the outing of pleasure for pleasure's sake. It's an odd shyness when you consider that part of God's alleged handiwork is that we're made for more than fruitfulness. The Lord who commanded Adam to multiply also gave Eve a clitoris. We are created in God's image, Scripture promises; therefore, it stands to reason that we are created not just for fruitfulness but for the giving and receiving of joy.

We'd lost our joy.

Looking back, that was what Ali was getting at around Hannah and Ryan's supper table. Like those straight-to-video Jean-Claude Van Damme movies with generic titles like *Out for Justice* that would work for a hundred different scripts, *Sad Fucking* could work as the title for a lot of marriages. Certainly it could work for every marriage at some point. Where a hickey evidences not only your appetite but its having been sated too, once you've come through it you can recognize the smooth scalp and neutropenic complexion of a cancer patient too. The look cancer leaves behind is the opposite of a hickey, marking the bruise that is your absence of appetite.

We'd had our own sad fucking, but I didn't have anyone's life in the balance to blame for it other than my own. Like a stroke's aphasia sandblasting words from its victim's mind and memory, my year of stage-serious chemo had eradicated my libido right along with my white blood cells. It left me both impotent and, to

1. Hi Mom, you can skip to chapter 6 now.

my eye at least, ugly. I looked and felt unrecognizably androgynous. I grasped for desire like wisps of half-remembered words. You don't realize how much a man's self-conception (rightly or wrongly) revolves around sex until it's snatched away from you. Without ability at it or appetite for it, cancer makes the carnal seem cruel.

When so much of your conscious mind is possessed by the knowledge that there's a killer loose in your body, it strikes you as a kind of assault to enter another's body. In the same way cunnilingus can inadvertently lead to a urinary tract infection (I've been told . . . by a friend), I was stalked by this irrational but stiffy-killing fear that I was contagious. Whenever we did try to go to bed together, always in the back of mind was the panic that Ali would get cancer from me if we got as close as bodies can get. In addition to being irrational, there was the very real near constant metallic twinge of nausea in the back of my mouth. It's hard to go down when you feel likely to throw up. When so much of your waking is given over to worrying about sharting, it's a stretch to feel sexy. Ali and I have never been ones for bedroom toys. Even if we were, the chemo pumps I carried attached to me for much of the time would not have counted. Pity is not conducive to desire. And while it's true that grief can make you randy, anticipatory grief (that is, fear) can kill the mood fast. It's hard to feel horny when you're taking herpes medication to ward off chemo-induced infection.

We'd tried some to give each other some during those days. In gentle, you-break-it-you-buy-it ways, with the lights off so that I couldn't see the fear in her eyes and she couldn't see the shame in my own, we'd try to reacquaint ourselves. Every time the anemia the chemo had effected in me left my heart racing and my head spinning. I could feel the worry in her body. She'd stop, holding me atop her. I'd hold on to her, hoping she wouldn't feel my tears hit her tense skin. And sure, I could do for her what I couldn't have done to me, with my hands and my mouth. But the inability for mutuality proved a mood killer, a little like inviting someone to come over to your house so they can watch you play with your toys.

Sex is tricky. In our culture we overvalue its currency. In the church we use it to draw ourselves on the right side of the righteousness equation. Yet no one seems to know how to speak about sex in the spiritual and psychic dimensions it demands. Good sex, when those dimensions are considered, requires more than the tips on technique Google can offer you. Two people can get no closer to each other than *in* each other, facing each other; therefore, a promise can get no more grave and no more graced than when it is a promise given in and with and under our bodies. Obviously, this is why there is no graver treason to a promise than when we betray it with our body. We identify with Peter denying Jesus as the cock crows. We empathize with him, and we loathe Judas who seals his lie with a kiss.

As a pastor, I've long mocked contemporary Christian music as the "Jesus Is My Boyfriend" genre of worship song. Too many of them sound like saccharine pop songs that simply traded out the name of a lover for Jesus. "Jesus, I'm so in love with you" is a chorus that comes to mind. But, perhaps there's something exactly right about those songs, even if it is unintentional. The medievals believed God doesn't see us when we make love. During sex, they insisted, the all-knowing, all-seeing Almighty absents himself. They were worse than silly in so thinking. The language of desire is the right language to speak of the God who made us, in his image, not only for offspring but for the offering of joy. The mystery called Trinity is disclosed to us most clearly in the Son making his life vulnerable to the Father, naked on a cross and trusting it to be returned with resurrection. This must mean that the mutual vulnerability of married sex is more than an attribute of love. It's our best analogy for how God loves God. We get no closer to the image of God than when we are happy and horizontal with one another.

Sex is more than a MacGuffin to the mystery of marriage. Sex isn't an intrigue that is ultimately incidental to our story's plot. Contrary to Christianity's deserved rep in the culture, our bodies are more than symptoms of Adam and Eve's error. The unabashedly erotic poem, the Song of Songs, contains a scene where the two lovers stand naked and unashamed before each other. The bride frankly admires her beau's boner. Seriously, it might offend you, but it's right there in the holy Bible wedged in between Ecclesiastes and Isaiah, like lingerie stuffed in between the gym socks and the pantyhose:

> My beloved thrust his hand into my opening, and my inmost being yearned for him. I arose to open to my beloved, and my hands dripped with myrrh, my fingers with liquid myrrh, upon the handles of his bolt.

In their joy and happy hunger for one another, the church has always seen in the lovers of the Song of Songs a parable, a story-formed image of the union between Christ and his church.

Bodies, then, are as essential to our nuptial promise as water is to baptism. Sex is inextricably the tangible means of your unconditional promise to another, no less than how the bread and wine that pass your lips are God's own offer of forgiveness.

When you get benched from bedroom play and your own body seems a stranger's, you notice just how embodied a faith Christianity is. It's more than the bread, wine, and water of the sacraments. It's how the word *peace* is incomplete without the feel of another's calloused hand in yours. It's how the dormant words on Scripture's page aren't the word of God until proclaimed out loud in front of others. It's how the singing of praise requires you to stand close enough to smell the stink on the breath of the person next to you. It's how membership among Jesus's people is membership *in his body*. The very language we use for the wedding bed is the language of the altar table, of consummation: bride and groom consume one another bodily. Only in so doing do they seal the promise made in the name of the God who did not count it a shameful act to assume our flesh. The consummation of the bride and groom's promise is a harbinger, the church proclaims, of the consummation of Christ's own promise to return for his bride, the church, his body.

In his essay "Big Red Son," David Foster Wallace relates the story of a Los Angeles detective, happily married and a grandpa, who had recovered a box of stolen porn films and, upon returning them to the film company, commented how strangely touching he'd found them. Despite being a law-and-order guy, he'd watched them. All of them. He confessed that what had transfixed him about them was the actresses' faces when, in reaching orgasm, the fake self they were portraying suddenly dropped like a veil, and you could see them in all their actuality and vulnerability. The "accidental humanness" of those precise moments of orgasm he found moving.

In recovering those videotapes, the detective had happened upon what the body of Christ has long considered the sacred nature of sex. At most, sex is a sacrament, the tangible sensory means of a couple's unconditional promise to one another, but at the very least, the mutual vulnerability and reciprocal joy of sex makes it a means of grace *in* our lives and an analogy *for* our lives to approximate God's own life as Father, Son, and Holy Spirit. The sudden absence of sex in a marriage can prove a loss not just of consortium but of communion. The betrayal of my own body, the loss of Ali's body to mine—I felt them like excommunications from Christ's own body, exorcisms of my faith. My lack of appetite left me starving for her, but also I was hungry for grace.

GRACE ISN'T ALWAYS GRACEFUL

There's no better place to make a fool of yourself than in the bedroom. And there's no likelier time you'll unwittingly play the role of a clown than when you've been on hiatus from rolling in the hay. It's hard to act cool when sex has once again taken on the ephemeral, mystical allure it had when you were a tween, watching *Adventures of the Gummi Bears* on NBC whilst thumbing through the Victoria's Secret catalogs that arrived like manna in your mother's mailbox. Just as every void and fissure is a place for grace to be deposited, wherever foolishness abounds in your life, Paul promises, Christ abides. If so, then, in the days after our cancer-induced celibacy, Jesus was in bed with us just as surely as God was incarnate in the folly of the cross. Christ was there between the sheets, pressed up near my pillow, to hear my every unspoken prayer. *Please, Jesus, don't let me mess this up. Help me, Lord, prove my manhood.*

Christians speak all the time of being born again. In doing so, we act as though it's an entirely envious experience. Christian culture even speaks of reclaiming one's lost virginity. But think about it: to reenter the world as blank as a baby is to repeat the awful awkwardness of adolescence. I had kissed those days goodbye. To learn again how to love with more than just my words struck me as about as welcome as transitioning once again through the crackling voice and pockmarked, acned skin of puberty. As every adolescent knows, sometimes the anxiety surrounding sex is more memorable than the act itself.

I'd missed her astride me, her head back, seeing her and being seen; the rush and bulge of blood through the vein in the side of her throat; the feel of the small of her back against my hand as she pressed against my abdomen; my mouth on her freckled hip looking down the length of her at the serene emptiness on her slight smile; her giggle as she took over, having judged the Chris Isaak video I was directing in my mind to have gone on long enough.

My first awareness of sex, at least that I can recall, I was standing in line at recess, waiting my turn at kickball. My friends Jason and Nathan were in front of me, my friends Megan and Elizabeth behind me. All of us were joking around, about what I do not remember. With no warning or introduction, Jason interrupted everyone to tell me that he and his parents had seen my dad "making out" with a woman in the parking lot of Bob Evans. "I bet they were having sex," Elizabeth shouted with calculated callousness. The others laughed. Megan was kind enough to ask if I knew and then told me she was sorry. Had I known what precisely sex was before that day, I'm sure I would've been scarred more by the mental association of coitus and the smell of breakfast sausages. As it was, I went home and looked it up in the old Encyclopedia Britannica my grandma had bequeathed me. I looked first in the slimmer Z volume. I thought she'd said "zex."

I suspect that because that moment is the trajectory from which I trace my own sexual awareness, sex from the beginning (and in the beginning of my own experience with it) got tied up with my fear of being left, a fear that became unrecognizable from a need to be needed. As a consequence, during the first few years of our marriage I was unable to let our lovemaking be play. Worse, I couldn't allow it to be clumsy. Still worse, I couldn't let it be ordinary. I needed to be needed so I needed *it* to be needed too. My need afflicted my love with a kind of performancism. In bed, I wasn't really present to her because I was busy portraying some unhelpful ideal in my mind. I was portraying a lover whose love would justify the choice she'd made in me. In my insecurity, I turned our bed into a gauntlet. In the bedroom, I felt expected to exhibit feats of longevity and lust that would make basic cable viewers blush. My need to live up to the porn star in my mind left us both exhausted rather than enraptured, frustrated instead of free. Sure, I was acting out of and reacting to my own particular story, but given all the unrealistic representations of sex our culture impresses upon us, teenage boys in particular, I do not think our first years of frustrated love were in any way unique.

To be a born-again virgin, post-chemo, was to endure all those unhelpful illusions again, and to victimize Ali with them. Coming out of my cancer-induced celibacy, I booked us a long winter weekend at the Château Frontenac in Quebec City, a palatial

French garrison overlooking the St. Lawrence River. You can only book a hotel where it's nine degrees outside if you don't plan to leave the room.

This is where the doors close and I draw the curtains. The details are ours. Let's just say that what I had in mind matched Kevin Costner's weekend tryst with Susan Sarandon in *Bull Durham*. I anticipated back-breaking, kitchen-table-smashing, rocking-the-water-out-of-the-tub animal passion.

Riding another is not like riding a bike.

Given the nightly rate I'd forked over, I was hoping for something like *9 1/2 Weeks* minus the lunchmeat. Instead it ended up being like the twenty-second wedding-night fadeout from *The 40-Year-Old Virgin*. On repeat. Only this version wasn't humorous. I felt humiliated, revisiting all my abiding insecurities of being left. Knowing she couldn't see the shame on my face but could feel the flushed heat of it, I laid my head, in surrender, on her bare shoulder. "It's okay," she said, "This is just where we're at right now, but we're in it together. We'll get through it. It doesn't make me love you any less, and it wouldn't have made me love you any more."

Maybe after falling in love you fail into it too. Maybe grace is never graceful. After all, grace can only come to us when it's unexpected. Grace, by definition, is always undeserved. Grace can only make us new when we've been knocked down. Forget lace and candlelight and long-stem roses. It turns out the naked acceptance of your naked, spent shame is sexier. It's the grace that's sexy. Maybe that's what the porny poem is doing in the Old Testament. In college I had a karate instructor who drilled into us his mantra, "Practice doesn't make perfect. *Perfect* practice makes perfect." Truth be told, he was kind of an asshole. He was also wrong, Christianly-speaking. Imperfect practice is perfect; the imperfect practice of a pair in lovemaking makes perfect. It's the imperfection, the acceptance and forgiveness in it, the grace of it, that comes the closest to the perfect love of God.

"It's like riding a bike. You just have to get back on until you find your balance."

GOD'S BEHIND

Every year around Holy Week people ask me "Why did Jesus have to die?" but the mystery with which the New Testament wrestles is not the *fact* of Jesus's death but the *manner* of that death. The point of the cross isn't the pain Christ suffered—that's why the Gospels say so little about it. The point of the cross is the *shame* Christ suffered.

Christ's manner of death made him exactly what he cries out with anguish: abandoned and accursed and ashamed.

Forsaken.

The shame is the point. The glory of God meets us not in our strivings up toward God but in our suffering and humiliation. The God who condescended to meet us in the crucified Christ never chooses any other avenue by which to meet us than condescension into suffering.

Luther said that Jesus Christ meets us so far down in the muck and mire of our lives that his skin smokes hot. God meets us in our shame and in our suffering. Only when we've been reduced to nothing do we know our need. You can't receive a gift in joy if you're determined it's unnecessary. As Luther continued in thesis 18 of the *Disputation*: "Man must utterly despair of his own ability before he is ready to receive grace." Knowing you have nothing to offer is the only way to receive what God has to give.

It's only when shit happens that you see you need a savior.

In his memoir *Mortal Lessons: Notes on the Art of Surgery*, Richard Selzer tells of a young woman, a new wife, from whose face he has removed a tumor, cutting a nerve in her cheek in the process and leaving her face smiling in a twisted palsy. Her young husband stands by the bed as she wakes and appraises her new self: "Will my mouth always be like this?" she asks.

The surgeon nods, and her husband smiles. "I like it," he says. "It is kind of cute."

Selzer goes one to testify to the epiphany he witnesses:

> All at once, I *know* who he is. I understand, and I lower my gaze. One is not bold in an encounter with God. Unmindful, he bends to kiss her crooked mouth, and I'm so close I can see how he twists his own lips to accommodate to hers, to show her that their kiss still works.[2]

The glory of God always shines forth in Jesus stooping over to kiss the shameful scabs and weeping wounds of lepers like us.

During their sojourn in the desert, still waiting on God to deliver the goods in the milk-and-honey department, Moses asks God to disclose his glory. "No one can see God's face and live," the Almighty explains to Moses before instructing him to hide in the cleft of a rock. As God passes by the rock, God covers Moses's eyes, permitting Moses only a glimpse of God's backside. God is the one who prevents Moses from seeing his glory. Whether from the cleft of a rock or upon a cross, God refuses to be seen in glory. To Moses, God gives only a peek at his behind. To us, God responds to our taunts at glory (If he's the Christ let him save himself!) by dying naked and accursed.

The gospel is a one-way story that goes down. The story of the cross is not the story of our journey up to God but God's journey down to us. Get the trajectory wrong and you're liable to point your mouth in the wrong direction when you cry out to God to save your marriage. You'll cry up into glory rather than down into the darkness you're in or out into the nothing and shadows that surround you.

When I first got the diagnosis of my slow drip, drip, drip death sentence, I reminded my parishioners over and over that "God's not behind this. God's not behind my cancer." And I believed it. I still do. The God who takes flesh in Jesus Christ to save us in his death doesn't do mean-ass shit to us just to get his rocks off.

---

2. Richard Selzer, *Mortal Lessons: Notes on the Art of Surgery* (San Diego: Harcourt Brace, 1996), 98.

The paradox of the theology of the cross is that though God is not behind my cancer, God is behind my cancer. That is, God is not behind my cancer in terms of culpability, but God *is* behind my cancer in terms of condescension. God wears my cancer and my limp-dick impotence and my shame like a mask.

Or like a wedding veil.

I'd never foist this disease on another. Yet, at the same time, I've found God hidden behind it. God has been present in what any other would perceive as absence, his skin smoking from sharing with me this pile-of-shit sickness. God refuses to be seen in any other way in our world than in *our* suffering and humiliation, *our* crosses, and *our* complicated conjugal beds. If the cross unmasks our spiritual pretension, then when the dying Christ declares, "It is finished," he ends any of our self-congratulatory projects that would have God be seen in any other way but in our need.

This reveals the danger in our sinful predilection for pretense in our marriages and relationships. When we refuse to own and acknowledge the problems between us, avoiding and denying the unhappiness, pretending we're okay and keeping up with the Joneses, we inadvertently tiptoe around the healing hiding there, to be discovered in our suffering.

Tying two sinners together forever is a time bomb waiting to go off. In marriage, of course, shit happens. The only way to overcome it is to go through it. That's because the savior is in it. Indeed, he's nowhere else but in it.

GETTING CAUGHT IN THE RAIN

We were driving to a movie with Ryan and Hannah, listening to the *Guardians of the Galaxy* soundtrack in the CD drive because it was Gabriel's latest obsession. Because his office is above the local movie house, Ryan and I double date every other week. Since getting cancer, we'd been on a string of accidentally seeing movies with unexpected cancer twists. When you're sick with it, you realize how often filmmakers use cancer as a plot device, from the science fiction flick *Arrival* to the *Rocky* reboot *Creed* to Guardians of the Freaking Galaxy.

The "Piña Colada Song" from Star Lord's *Awesome Mix Volume I* started to play. In the movie, it plays while Rocket Racoon and company escape from a galactic prison. At a red light, I listened to the lyrics of this supposed love song for the first time.

"Have you ever paid attention to these lyrics before?" I asked them all.

"What's that?" Ryan asked.

"This song, 'If you like piña coladas and walks in the rain,' it's about a married couple nearly committing adultery."

"Holy shit, really? I never really listened. I just figured it was another awful yacht-rock song."

"No, listen to it," I said, turning it up, "It's like *Fatal Attraction* with coconut instead of crazy."

It's true. The song's original title is "Escape."

As in, from marriage.

The man and wife of Rupert Holmes's 1979 number-one hit song flip about forsaking everything they promised one another. Each of them, unsuspecting of the other, takes out a Want Ad, searching for someone who is perfect for them, a companion who likes the feel of the ocean and the taste of champagne. Only, in the end, the husband discovers that the woman who's answered his ad is his "lovely old lady."

"I bet calling his wife 'lovely old lady' didn't help their marriage," Ryan laughed.

It's a song about two imperfect people on the precipice, their marriage near nothing.

And if you pay attention to the lyrics, there's an ironic twist on what we mean by the term *soul mate*, for when the imperfect spouses meet each other through the want ads, what do they do? They laugh.

They say: "I never knew that you like piña coladas . . ."

And then they laugh. Each of them laughs at the imperfect other.

"Listen to it again," I said. The light changed to green as I pressed the left arrow on the stereo. "Their marriage has gotten so bad they're taking out want ads. Both of them are found out nearly destroying their marriage and then they just laugh about it. I mean, what are the chances you'd be laughing?"

"It would take a miracle," Ali answered.

Ryan smacked his hands together, laughing.

She was being sarcastic, but she was as right as the rain the couple like getting caught in. The "Piña Colada Song" only works as a contemporary Christian song. The only thing that makes Rupert Holmes's love song work is the cross. The only thing that makes their happy, forgiving laughter believable is the God who has met us in our suffering found us out in our deepest failures, and by the happy joke we call Easter, laughed.

Without such a God, *all* our love songs would be break-up songs.

CHAPTER 6.

IN THE NUDE

Spare us the indignity of indiscriminate acceptance.
—Robert Capon, *Between Noon and Three*

The shortest distance between two people is laughter.
—Me, stealing that line from someone

That's stupid. You're an idiot.
—Ali, speaking the truth in love

UNDERCOVER LESBIAN EVANGELISM

"Your problem is in thinking that God is somewhere other than right here in a place like this," I said.

I was sitting at the infusion center near the hospital receiving my latest monthly maintenance chemo to keep the cancer at bay. *What the hell*, I thought to myself, finding a copy of my book *Cancer Is Funny* stashed behind old copies of *Redbook* and *People*. I pulled it out and read the illegible name scrawled on the inside page and darkly thought *They better have had a cancer emergency that explains them forgetting my book behind.*

I tossed it onto the seat across from me where a few minutes later another patient sat down and began to thumb through it before looking at the head shot on the dust jacket and then glancing over at me, looking me over with the stink eye.

"I'm kind of a big deal," I said to her.

"Yeah?"

I smiled and shook my head. "No, not at all."

If I'd known that later that evening I'd be in our master bathroom, rooting through the trashcan for tampon wrappers, convinced that that time of the month had visited Ali and that it was the only explanation for our angry row, then I would've wiped the smartass smile from my face.

On one of the two TVs in the infusion lab, every commercial break—I'm not exaggerating—featured an advertisement from Lexington Plastic Surgeons, who, according to the voiceover pitchman, have more offices around the country than Skynet in the *Terminator* films.

"Do you think I'd look good if I got a Brazilian Butt Lift?" I asked my nurse as she pressed and then taped the needle down against my arm.

And for the record, yes, I suppose I was flirting.

"Um . . . maybe?" she replied. "You're not really my type, butt lift or no butt lift."

The other TV in the lab was playing Rachael Ray's cooking show. Every commercial break of Rachael's show featured a spot selling Rachael Ray's own line of boutique dog food, which if you're counting at home is reason #93 to hate Rachael Ray.

"Do you think it's strange that in between recipes for people food, Rachael Ray is also selling dog food? I mean, are those transferable skills?" I asked my nurse.

She laughed as she hung my bag of pre-meds. She had short, buzzed hair dyed a turquoise that matched the gem stud in her nostril and complemented the purple cat-eye glasses on her nose. Looking at the tattoos on my arm, she told me that her girlfriend was a tattoo artist.

"We're thinking of getting married, my girlfriend and me," she said. "You're a priest, right? You gotta be with tattoos like those. You probably think we're sinners?" She was asking, not accusing.

"If you're going to ask me these sorts of questions, I think you should return my copay." But she just sat on the wheeled stool next to me, waiting.

"Sinners? Yes." I said.

And then added: "But no more than me."

She looked confused, like what I'd said wasn't as bad as she'd feared and not as good as she'd hoped.

"Look," I said, "It's a simple formula I've heard: People are sinners. Christians are people. Christians are sinners. So yeah, no more than me."

She nodded and flicked the tube to start the drip.

Another commercial from Skynet came on the television, this one for breast augmentation and eyebrow lifts and wrinkle removing along with a lie about defying time and aging.

"It's kind of a waste of their ad budget to have their commercials played in here, don't you think?"

"What do you mean?"

"I mean, it's kind of obvious and unavoidable here that nobody is getting out of life alive, but that's exactly what Skynet is promising."

"Skynet?"

"Never mind."

She smoothed out my crinkled chemo tube and she asked me: "Do you ever wonder where God is, considering . . . your situation?"

Now it was my turn to stare and study her.

"I see a lot of people lose their faith in a place like this. I guess it can be hard to believe there's a god somewhere in the universe when there's places like this in it too."

"Your problem," I said, "is in thinking that God is somewhere other than right here in a place like this."

She squinted, like she was weighing whether I was shoveling BS or saying something true. She handed me a little plastic cup of pills (meds to minimize the tremors the chemo causes), and she said, "Can I ask you, since you brought it up, if you died—or, when you die—do you know where you'll go?"

"What are you?" I asked, "Some sort of undercover lesbian evangelist?"

She smiled just a little, "No, I've just never been that religious and I don't know how you know, you know, that you'll go to heaven or be with God or whatever."

I nodded yes.

"You're certain?" she asked me. She was studying me, the way she did at the end of infusions to make sure I was okay to drive home.

I nodded again, vaguely embarrassed at the looks I was getting from the other patients.

"You're really certain?"

So I said it: "Yes."

"How can you be so sure? How can you have that much faith?"

I shrugged my shoulders and I said: "I dunno." Seriously, I said: "I dunno." A question like that about faith and heaven and eternal life should be my Bible bread and butter, but the best I could do was shrug my shoulders and fart out an "I dunno." No wonder Young Life rejected me as a leader in college. I get paid a salary and benefits—too much, some geezers in my congregation gripe—but someone asks me point blank about faith and heaven and eternal life and the best I can do is shrug my shoulders and say, "I dunno." I was so inarticulate with her you'd think it would take a miracle for me to give her the gospel.

"Do you think about it much?" she asked, smoothing out the tape anchoring the chemo needle into my arm, "Dying?"

The late theologian Robert Jenson argued that it was impossible for the mind of the creature to comprehend the moment of its mortality drawing to a final close. We can imagine the loved ones gathered around or the screech of the car's brakes or the blips on the hospital monitor. We can even see the warm white light at the end of the tunnel, but we cannot conceive the moment of death itself, creatures cannot conjure knowledge that belongs exclusively to the Creator. Maybe Jenson was right about death, and it explains why I'd become preoccupied with daydreaming not about my death but about my funeral. Of course, another possible explanation to add to Jenson's is that I'm a narcissist.

Do I think about dying? Some, I suppose. Honestly, I think more about my funeral.

It's true. I daydream a lot about my funeral. I visualize the whole service, starting with the bouquets. I know it's popular nowadays to request that, in lieu of flowers, money be sent to this or that charity. Not me. In the funeral in my mind, the church sanctuary room is wearing more flora than Brooke Shields in *The Blue Lagoon*. I mean, giving to charity is about other people. I've lived my whole life as if it's all about me; at least in death it really will be. And so in my daydream friends and acquaintances all send so many flowers the sanctuary looks like *FTD* exploded all over it.

In my daydream there's flowers all over and the pews are packed, and it's standing room only in the lobby. It's so crowded that Sasha and Malia have to sit on their dad's lap, and everyone nods in approval when Pope Francis gets up to offer his seat to Cindy Crawford. When it comes time for the processional, Pastor Dennis, his voice cracked and ragged from raging Job-like at the heavens, invites everyone to stand. And in that moment my boys actually stop playing on their iPads and carry in my casket. As my casket is brought forward toward the altar, the organist plays the music from the scene in *Star Wars Episode IV* where Han and Luke (but not Chewy, for some ethnocentric reason) receive their medals.

Once I'm brought forward in front of the altar table, all those curmudgeons from my congregation who were never without a complaint about me kneel before my casket and quietly confess their many sins against me and beg me not to haunt them. Then, they're followed by a long line of women in veils and stilettos who all look like the bride in the "November Rain" video. They come forward, each to lay a rose on my casket, and each of them behind her veil wears an expression that seems to say, "You were a man among boys, Jason."

As the pastor begins with his lines about the resurrection and the life, the bishop slinks into the sanctuary embarrassed to be running late and squeezes into a spot in the back corner where the late Stephen Hawking assures him in his Speak & Spell voice that it's just getting started.

When the pastor gets up to preach, because he's nervous to preach in front of the Dalai Lama, he fumbles with his notes. But then he is overcome with emotion, so he hands his notes to his associate, and she stands up in the pulpit and, first, she reads the Gospel passage, the centurion at Christ's cross: "Truly, this was God's Son." And then she looks down at the pastor's notes and reads what he has prepared: "While these words normally refer to Jesus, I think we can all agree that in Jason's case . . ."

After the sermon, which in my daydream does a thorough job of quoting my own sermons, the choir comes to the front, wearing brand-new robes that have my likeness on the back in sequins. The choir is led by a special guest vocalist, and together they pay me tribute by singing the Gladys Knight cover of "Best Thing That Ever Happened to Me." Despite the heavyset black woman leading them, the choir veers off key because the choir director's eyes are filled with angry, manstrating tears and he can't see his music to conduct it. So the choir's singing their hearts out and even though they're singing off-key, Scarlett Johansson leans over and asks Penélope Cruz for a tissue to dab her teared eyes just as the choir belts out the final line: "I know, you're the best thing, oh, that ever happened to me."

After the applause dies down, Ali chokes back her tears and anguish, and she steps up to the lectern to eulogize me. She starts by pointing out how she knew me longer than anyone, from the time she saw me in my Speedo at swim practice, which is to say it was love at first sight.

"So I just want to say," Ali concludes and wipes her eye, "Jason was mostly an okay guy."

With that, she steps down and afterward there's no closing hymn or benediction, no "Amazing Grace" or Lord's Prayer, because at some point during the prayer of commendation the roof is rent asunder as at the transfiguration, and God the Father declares "This is my Beloved in whom I am well pleased." Jesus and the Holy Spirit descend from the clouds, along with the ghosts of Mother Teresa, Dumbledore, Gandalf, and Leonard Nimoy, and together they carry me, like the prophet Elijah, up into the heavens.

And so, then, there's nothing else to do but go to the fellowship hall where the stage is lined with kegs of 90 Minute IPA, where my boys are back to playing on their tablets, and where the food is piled high around a giant ice sculpture. Of me.

"You really think about your funeral?" the nurse asked me.

"Oh, um, just a little," I said and then filled her in on some of the details of my daydream.

"That's kind of funny."

"Kind of? Screw you."

"It *is* funny. You tell your wife about your daydream?"

I shook my head.

She didn't say anything more about it. I took it as a suggestion. As in, *That's really funny. You should share that with your wife.*

I'm a moron.

FORGET THE AMISH

The downside of having published a book with the word "funny" in its title is that it officially credentials me as a comedian. It validates my worst inclination to assume every word out of my mouth is goddamned hilarious. "Don't encourage him," is one of

Ali's mantras, and it's worn down smooth as a seaside pebble from so much use. She's not always joking when she says it.

Later that evening, still nauseous from the maintenance chemo, I was making dinner in the kitchen, cutting vegetables to be thrown in with the chicken roasting in the oven. Just home from work, Ali was sitting on the kitchen counter, as she likes to do, still in her lawyer's costume. Her heels were off, and her feet were perched on the island. I reached into the cabinet above her for something I pretended to need. Suggestively I slid my other hand down her leg and up her skirt. She rolled her eyes and kissed me anyways.

"Back off, mister. I'm hungry."

"I'm hungry too," raising my eyebrow into a come-hither arch and beat-boxing my best porn soundtrack.

"Yeah, no. Too bad."

She was smiling. I took that as a small victory.

Encouraged, I told her about my nurse and how I'd told her about my funeral daydream and how hilarious she'd found it. How hilarious she'd found me. Assuming she'd want to hear it herself, I launched into all of it, performing it like a stand-up doing a bit.

It didn't kill.

It hurt.

The silence got me to look up from the cutting board. Her face was already splotchy red. Tears she didn't bother to wipe away dripped from her eyes. She exhaled in short measured breaths like she does when she's trying not to cry.

I put the knife down.

"Geez, I was just joking." For some asinine reason (I'm a dunderheaded asshat is the reason), I thought that was a good response.

"It's not a joke. It's not funny. It's not anything but . . ."

Dammit, the nurse was implying I NOT tell my wife. Crap, I'm an idiot, I thought to myself.

I started to move toward her. To hug it away so I could get back to shits and giggles. She flashed me a look and I knew to step back. Then I saw true sorrow flash across her face. And I felt ashamed.

She exploded.

The truth of us exploded all over me:

I work too many hours in a job I hate. I'm stuck there because if I take time away from it I won't be able to go back to it. And I'll need to go back to it because you're *going* to get sick again. All I can think about all the time is how I'm probably going to be a widow before I'm forty-five. I start sobbing at random all the time—my coworkers probably think I'm crazy. Our kids are depressed. I go to church where everyone wants to talk about what a miracle it is you're *healed*. It's not funny. There's no fucking funny in any of it.

I gulped.

"I'm sorry, honey."

"And you're so glad to be feeling better and be back to work, you don't bother to engage *how I feel*. The grief didn't go away. It just turned to dread."

"It's just . . . I'm afraid to think about it, the future, so I avoid asking you about it either," I attempted to explain. "I'm sorry."

I could feel every second she didn't speak.

"I forgive you."

"What can I do?"

"Nothing," she sighed and wiped her eyes. "There's nothing you need to do, babe."

"Do you want to talk about it?"

She shook her head.

"Do you want to tell me how you feel?"

She shook me off.

It's disarming to be told there's nothing for you to do. It dislodges you from the ground in which you've dug your heels to handle whatever comes your way.

"Do you want to tell me what you're going through? I can stop making cancer jokes. I can start checking in on how you're feeling more. Tell me, what should I do?"

"There's nothing you need to do but shut up and listen: I FORGIVE YOU." She'd raised her voice but not because she was angry. She was being emphatic.

"But . . ." the word dribbled out of me like a last resort. "I gotta make this right, right?"

"No, I forgive you. End of story." She was attempting to smile, getting back to the playful self she'd been before I screwed things up.

"There's gotta be *something* I can do."

She shook her head and wiped her eyes on her sleeve. "No, then it would depend on you doing something instead of on me forgiving you. You don't get to be in charge of how I feel about you."

I went back to crushing garlic with the side of my chef's knife. "I don't deserve it."

"Nope," she said. "But it's yours all the same."

Forget the Amish with their seventy times seven forgiveness; seventy times seven just puts them in the driver's seat of their horse-drawn buggy. It's harder to be forgiven than it is to forgive. Being forgiven feels like suffering. It feels like dying, the Old Adam in you flatlining.

I bit my lip and then sucked at my teeth like I do when I'm angry.

I was angry. "There's gotta be SOMETHING I *need* to do."

It's odd. She'd forgiven me unconditionally and completely gratuitously, and I felt attacked by it. I was the one angry now.

"There's *gotta* be something."

"No," she said.

Being forgiven—it bleeds the ledger into another's account. It might wipe your slate clean, but your memory of what was written there abides. To have your debt paid, gratis, is to grapple with a different kind of owing. Forgiveness is not a monotone word.

Forgiveness is a word that kills as much as it makes alive. Accusation always precedes pardon in our ears. To hear "I forgive you of your sins" is to hear that you're a sinner. We rush to respond to our forgiven-ness in order to right the scales and to restore the balance of power. A system of merits and demerits, a quo for every quid, comforts the Old Adam in us who is addicted to control.

"FINE. I won't do any damn thing then. Screw it."

I slammed the oven door. I threw the oven mitt across the kitchen, knocking a metal spatula off the island and startling the dog. Thank God, the kids were at swim practice. I grabbed my keys and I left—early—to pick them up. I shut the front door so hard, I heard the force of it suck the back kitchen door closed.

There's a Korean movie I saw a few years back called *Secret Sunshine*. In the film, a widow relocates to the village of her dead husband only to see their son murdered. She later channels her grief into her faith and works up the gumption to visit her son's killer in prison in order to bestow forgiveness on him. Really, she's found Christianity a useful channel to wield forgiveness as a weapon against her son's victimizer. When they meet, the killer surprises her with the shock of the gospel. He too has become a Christian and, with the zeal of a prison convert who's convinced the riches of heaven are his to own and bestow, he wants her to know that she is forgiven, too. There to accuse more than offer forgiveness, she finds herself feeling attacked by his forgiveness.

Without an assist from subtitles, I drove to swim practice that night finally understanding the movie.

NUDE FAITH

"Saying sorry doesn't cut it," my mom used to tell me. "You've got to earn forgiveness." As a kid, my mother saying "sorry doesn't cut it" cut me. It sounded harsh, but as a husband I've realized free forgiveness can feel harder and can cut deeper. To be in the right with another, we assume, you've got to do right by them—seek restitution, make reparations, repair the damage you did. Not only does saying "sorry doesn't cut it" make sense to us (it's how we've arranged the world), it actually gives us more control than does the free offer of forgiveness. *To be in the right with another is to do right by them* might put me on somebody's shit list, but it at least leaves me in the driver's seat for what will follow; whereas, *to be in the right with another is to be declared right by them* takes away everything from me and leaves me empty-handed. Faith alone in your promise of forgiveness is a disavowal of my own performance to merit it.

If I have to earn your forgiveness, then at least I'll accrue evidence external to either of us to which I can point and justify myself later. If I have to earn your pardon, then I can simultaneously be on the lookout for anything I can use as leverage against you should you withhold forgiveness. *Look at all that I did to make it up to you and still it wasn't enough,* I've griped to more than just my wife. But if forgiveness is free, then, like on my wedding day, I've got absolutely nothing to hold onto but you. I've got nothing to hold on to but my trust in you.

Those who mimic Christ's unconditional promise by marrying one another in his name take a bigger risk than they realize. Those who say "I do" agree to forget how to count. Bride and groom not only forsake all others from their bed and their hearts, they forsake the calculators we all carry with us and with which we balance the sums and subtractions of our relationships. We're left on our wedding day with no recourse but to take the other at their word. To trust that you forgive me is to have faith you won't use my debt later to burn me.

Forgiveness isn't cheap, Robert Capon says. It isn't even expensive. It's free.

Yet the bitter irony that makes every marriage a beautiful risk is that this free forgiveness could cost you everything. More so than the person with whom you share your bed, the graver risk of fidelity in marriage is letting your lover's promise of forgiveness leave you empty-handed. In marriage you trust that, having been forgiven of it, your wrongdoing won't boomerang back onto you. You trust your lover won't wield your wrong later as a weapon against you.

We didn't talk about it when I brought the boys home from swim practice.

I'm not proud of it, but in my pride I needed to find a reason Ali had (over)reacted so emotionally to a stupid story. Closing the front door behind me, I crept upstairs to our bathroom and rummaged, like our dog does, through the trashcan looking for the torn-off bits of tampon wrapper that would plead my case.

It was not one of my prouder moments.

Finding nothing, I finished dinner. I set the table. I served it with loud and demonstrative clanking of plates and shutting of drawers. All the noise was designed to continue the monologue I'd launched into when I'd thrown the oven mitt across the kitchen. Talk at the dinner table was tight and polite: *How was your day at school? What did you learn in class? What homework do you still have to do?*

After dinner, Ali helped with homework. She put the boys to bed while I put away the dishes and cleaned up. She started to watch a SYFY show upstairs in our bedroom. I started to concoct chores downstairs in order to avoid going upstairs. Or, really, I suppose I was passive-aggressively waiting for her to come downstairs. *Apologize to me!* the attorney in my mind relitigated the argument. Knocking shit around downstairs for no reason, I preferred to provoke another argument. I needed—I use that word intentionally, I *needed*—to have the scales evened between us.

I did not want to receive her free forgiveness, which felt like an IOU.

I fell asleep reading at the kitchen table. When I woke up, I could hear the TV still on in the bedroom. Underneath what sounded like a cheesy space show, I could hear Gabriel whimpering in his sleep. By the time I started up the stairs, he was crying, still asleep. It woke Ali up too. We both laid down next to him. Both of us on either side of his skinny twin bed. Ali shushed him. I gently combed his sweaty hair, mussed across his forehead, with my hand.

"What's the matter, sweetie?" she asked, kissing his ear. "Did you have a bad dream?"

He suddenly clenched his eyes shut like he does in scary movies and nodded his head.

"It's okay, honey," Ali whispered. "It was just a nightmare."

Whether it was the *just* or the *nightmare*, the levy broke, and he started to sob so hard he couldn't catch his breath. I put my hand underneath his *Prairie Home Companion* T-shirt and rubbed his back.

"It's okay, buddy," I said.

His frantic exhales sounded like the kickback on a gun until, finally, he could blurt out what he'd been mustering: "It's *not okay*! I had a dream that you got sick again and died."

Then his cries turned to inconsolable hiccups. I buried his head in the crook of my arm and chest so he couldn't see me crying. I could feel Ali on the other side of the slim IKEA bed trying not to hyperventilate like him. For several minutes I rubbed his back and reassured him "that's not going to happen any time soon. I promise buddy."

Over and over.

"That's not going to happen any time soon. I promise buddy."

Until he'd stopped crying and had calmed down.

Then I said, "That's not going to happen any time soon. I promise buddy. Besides, if I did die you'd get all my albums."

As soon as I'd cast it out as a joke, I wanted to reel it back onto the spool.

But Ali laughed instead. And although I could tell it was a forced laugh, it felt like grace.

"Your dad has a lot of albums," she giggled. "Which would be your top five?"

Gabriel nodded and wiped the snot from his nose. As if beginning to answer her question, he said "Alexa, play David Bowie."

Ground control started calling for Major Tom.

"Dad?"

"Yeah, buddy?"

"If you die . . ." held the pause like a budding stand-up.

"If you die can I have your iPad too?"

"Um . . . uh . . ."

"Got you!" he smiled and then patted my back as though I was the one who needed consoling. "Don't die old man *until you're an old man*."

"You got it buddy."

A BUNCH OF BALONEY

Gabriel had smiled and joked again about wanting to inherit my pocket knife, too, should my inevitable end hasten its arrival. I kissed him. He reassured me as I pulled his door ajar enough for the bathroom light to spill across the threshold: "Just kidding, Dad, I want you more than a crummy pocket knife." And he let out a last little giggle as he rolled over, turning his back to the darkness.

As Ali fell asleep spooned against me, her breath blowing on my chest (she's always been a mouth-breather), I wondered if Gabriel would have found any of it funny had he been home earlier. Would he have made jokes about my death if he'd heard his mother's hurt? Would he have laughed if he'd seen her grief explode out of her with such apocalyptic force? Or would all my joking have left him angry too?

I remember the night when I was a little younger than Gabriel. My dad, drunk, had backed into the tree along our long narrow gravel driveway. Such was the pretense we kept as a family, I feigned a deep sleep through it all. I'd heard him fumbling in his dresser downstairs. I'd heard him knocking cartons around in the refrigerator. Then the garage door opened and the car door shut and the engine revved. Even after I heard the muffled thud and the car crumple against the oak tree, I continued to fake sleep. I didn't rise to pull up the blind. I didn't look out the window. I knew. A few minutes passed. Then I heard the car creep up the driveway, sheepish and ashamed.

The next morning I was breaking eggs for French toast. My dad was snoring on the couch. My mom came home from her shift at the hospital. I'd already been outside to look at the bruised and stripped tree in our front yard. Pieces of my father's taillight were embedded in the wood and scattered in the driveway like my Lego pieces on the basement floor. My mom woke up my dad. In their bedroom, which was adjacent to the kitchen, she started questioning him in tones too big for the hush they were attempting. A few minutes later she came into the kitchen and helped me to batter the pieces of bread; my dad smoked a cigarette at the kitchen table.

I guess it was a spiteful curiosity that compelled me to interrogate them. Like a little shit, I decided to play the bad cop *playing the good dumb cop*.

"I heard a loud crash last night and the tree outside is all messed up now and there's bits of the car's lights everywhere."

I was baiting them into a lie.

"Your dad's window was frosted up, he couldn't see very well," my mom answered quickly.

"But, where was he going in the middle of the night after we'd gone to bed?"

"Left something at work. I was too lazy to scrape the windows," he said, blowing smoke.

I left it. We all left it. It was another broken eggshell on the floor we'd learn to tiptoe around until the lie about the frosted window would become true, like a rosary, simply through religious repetition. Later, we'd even make jokes about his laziness and forgetfulness when it came to scraping winter windows.

We all aided and abetted the charade.

Sometime later my dad took off. Without warning (not like there weren't warning signs), he went away with another woman to Singer Island. His week-long tryst left us with little food in the fridge and no cash in the bank.

My mom got us through my dad's seaside sojourn by buying us food at the gas station with her Super America credit card. To this day, I hate the smell of baloney. I remember thinking that surely this would prove the fatal crack in our charade, an irredeemable breech that would force my mother's hand. She'd forsake him once and for all.

Instead she forgave him.

Sitting on the top of the stairs outside my bedroom, I heard him pleading and promising in their bedroom downstairs. Later, they announced to us that they would be leaving together on a short vacation of their own. I couldn't believe it. And, I feared more damn baloney.

"He's promised to do better by us," my mom said, trying to tamp down my fury.

"That's a bunch of baloney," I shouted, and then thinking of our convenience store menu: "Baloney!?"

"He's very sorry for everything."

"Sorry doesn't *FUCKING* cut it."

It was my first curse.

When your mom works nights and your dad is in absentia, you can sneak a lot of cable. Latchkey kids learn a lot of vocabulary words. It never occurred to me that my mom understood then what I did not. She understood how every one of his apologies and pleas to do better by us were sincere, such is bondage of addiction.

My sister and I went to stay at our aunt's, whose spurious comments about how much fun my parents must be having in Florida only infuriated me all the more over the flow of free forgiveness that kept coming his undeserved way. Only later was I able to articulate how I was angrier at her for giving out such free and foolish forgiveness than I was at him for getting it.

SORRY CUTS IT

Not every wound heals. And unless God is the giver, free, one-way grace is no guarantee to get you to happily ever after. Eventually my parents' divorce was really more of an acknowledgement of what was broken beyond repair. Their divorce simply announced that their marriage was like a house that gets razed rather than rebuilt after a tree that proves too big has collapsed onto it.

Back then as a kid, I was irate over her willingness to forgive him freely. Today, as a pastor who enjoys some discretion over who gets to say "I do," I don't say yes to any couple who isn't willing to do just like her. It's not because I naïvely think that everything broken can be mended. It can't. All that *Chicken Soup for the Soul* and *Proverbs 31 Woman* is crap. Not every problem can be prayed away or solved by being an awesome wife. I'm certainly not one of those hair-sprayed Neanderthal clergy who think an authentically Christian spouse must grin and bear any abuse. No, the reason I insist that the couples over whose nuptials I preside are people of faith is because they need to believe that the call and response of repentance and forgiveness is the only way they will be changed. I use the passive voice on purpose. The call and response of *I'm sorry/You're forgiven* is the liturgy of married life. It's the back-and-forth of bride and groom by which God sanctifies us.

Offering forgiveness freely and freely receiving it, we are made holy. We do not grow closer to God or grow more like God through improvement. The language of spiritual progress implies a gradual lessening of our need for grace the nearer and nearer we journey to God. Yet, the God who condescends to us in the suffering, humble, and humiliated Christ is not ever a God waiting for us to make our way up to him. The God who came down to meet us in crèche and cross continues to forsake his lofty throne. God comes down still. He hides behind unimpressive words like, "I forgive you."

God changes us through the ordinary means of "I'm sorry" and "I forgive you." As much as water, wine, and bread, your wife's free offer of forgiveness in the face of your sin is a sacrament of God's transforming grace. The Beloved gets no closer to us than our bride or our groom. The Bridegroom has condescended to us whenever we see our sin in the eyes of our beloved yet hear instead words of unmerited pardon. God not only wears these words of forgiveness like flesh, God uses them to transform us. This is why, to every prospective husband and wife who gushingly tell me how they've found their soul mate, I've practiced responding, "Big deal."

We have so much in common.

"Big deal."

She's just like me in every way.

"Big deal."

We fit together like two puzzle pieces. [People actually talk like this.]

"Big deal."

We're so compatible.

"Big deal."

Don't get me wrong, compatibility sounds awesome. The language of compatibility makes marriage sound easy. The problem my unimpressed "big deal" is meant to unveil is that, to the extent Christian marriage is meant to be a parable of God's own love, change does not come through compatibility. Change, Christianly speaking, comes through collision. We are not transformed by seamlessly fitting another into our life. We're not all puzzle pieces strewn across the great cosmic game table. Sorry, no one is *The One* for you. Another can only become *The One* for you as you are both made holy. And holiness comes through the rough-and-tumble process of having another reveal our true sucky self to us.

Before we're married, not only do we have an incomplete understanding of the other person. We have an incomplete understanding of our selves. We bring in to marriage a self-image that's been formed by the judgments and praise of people who don't know us as well as our spouse eventually will know us; consequently, as we live our lives with someone else, we discover that we're not the same person we thought we were. And in a marriage, there's not a lot of room to hide. You're exposed. All the veils are pulled away. It's not that there's no secrets in marriage. It's that there aren't as many secrets as we want.

It's the inverse of what I like to call Jason's Rule, which is really a cribbed version of Hauerwas's Rule. Jason's Rule states that *You never really know the person you're marrying until after you've been married to the person you're marrying.* The corollary to Jason's Rule is that *You are never as fully known as you are known by the person to whom you're married.* So once you're inside a marriage, it's not just the other person's flaws and imperfections that are revealed. It's your own.

But notice, it's not your spouse who's unveiling your flaws and imperfections. It's marriage. This is what collared types like me mean when we call marriage "a means of God's grace." It's a means by which God condescends to us to convict us and to change us. Our true self must be revealed through the painful process occasioned by the need to say "I'm sorry" so that through his word of free pardon, God can unveil, by degrees, our transformed self.

DIE EVERY DAY

My mom was wrong.

Dropping my first F-bomb as a kid, I was wrong too. Saying

sorry *does* cut it. It's the way in which God cuts away all the bits that are not us.

We kissed Gabriel goodnight and turned off the lights and stripped and went to bed, our fingers crossed that all would be well with him.

"I'm sorry," I said, stroking her hair. "I didn't mean to make another joke about it."

She could have thrown it all back in my face, rehearsing the fight we'd had hours earlier and every other fight whence it came. Such reenactments between couples easily and quickly become the habits ingrained in their marriage. Honestly, that's exactly what I deserved. I'd not only done to her what I'd just promised not to do to her, but, had he not taken the cue and run with it, I would've done it to Gabriel too.

"I'm sorry," I said again when she didn't answer.

"I know," she said and kissed me.

Then she told me she forgave me. Where before I would've pressed, cloying and insecure, this time I left it alone. What can be a scary question at the beginning of a marriage (Are you the same person I married?) is the very best thing a husband and wife can ever say to each other at the end or, fingers crossed, somewhere in the middle. "I'm not the person you married. Thank you."

I had the wrong answer to the lesbian nurse evangelist's question from the get-go. Do I think about dying? I should've told her: I screw up and suck all the time, yet I'm forgiven every time.

Which is to say, I die every day.

On Gabriel's Alexa, David Bowie had left Major Tom behind and was now wondering if there was life on Mars.

CHAPTER 7.

THE MORNING AFTER

There is a time in life when a man with a little acting ability is able to deceive even himself.

—Graham Greene, *A Burnt Out Case*

Expectations are the enemies of love.

—Alain de Botton

A SOUND LIKE SOMEONE TRYING NOT TO MAKE A SOUND

When Gabriel was a little boy, his favorite story book was *A Sound Like Someone Trying Not to Make a Sound* by John Irving. It's actually an excerpt from his adult novel, *A Widow for One Year*, in which the main character's father is a children's author and illustrator. *A Sound Like Someone Trying Not to Make a Sound* is one of the fictional father's stories that Irving later published and illustrated as a stand-alone children's book. It's a spare and frightening story of a little boy waking up in the still of the night to a sound between the walls of his bedroom.

Gabriel loved it the way you love a horror movie for the thrill of panic and the comfort of relief it gives you at the end. When he was in the second grade, I read it to his class. Crocodile tears and cranky emails from kids' parents followed, because it's a story about dread, a story about imagining the worst lurking, like a shadow—always out of reach, ever ready to pounce.

Ali had tried talking to me about it. I wouldn't listen. Not until she packed her suitcase one afternoon because nothing else would get my attention. Ali had warned me. I was too much of a coward to admit it or engage it. Since I'd gotten sick, Gabriel had started hiding a shadow side to his self too.

His jokes were sarcastic masks behind which he hid from the dread that stalked him until finally he, like Irving's little boy, was sleepless and spent. His fear of my death was the sound ringing not between the walls but between his ears. He exhausted himself trying to muffle it. Then, exhausted, he didn't want to do it anymore.

And, like the little boy in the story, he tiptoed into the dark.

A week after he was cracking jokes about inheriting my iPad when I kicked the bucket, we got a phone call from the school psychologist. During a screening for Attention Deficit Disorder, which we'd requested, Gabriel had confided to her: he'd been thinking about suicide.

Friends in his class confirmed that he'd talked to them about ending his own life.

After getting the call, I went to pick up Gabriel early from school. "We can only release him to a guardian," the school psychologist had explained with no affect. Driving to the school, I sat too long at a light and missed it as it turned from red to green and back again to red, staring blankly, sifting through the shards of memories until I could recall his name. *Jackson.*

Almost ten years earlier, I'd gotten a call that one of our eleven-year-old confirmands was in the ER at Mt. Vernon Hospital. Maybe he was already dead, a parishioner told me on the phone.

When I got there, he was gone. Jackson's mom was on the bed with her arms around him and was telling him how much she loved him, how much everyone loved him. Jackson's grandpa, a rough four-star general, had his arms around her. Blanketing her wailing with sobs too deep for words. For I don't know how long, I held Jack's hand and rubbed his hair and tried to get the words out. I tried to tell him how funny and special and alive I thought he was. It wasn't until his mom sat up and asked me to pray that I noticed the ligature marks around his neck.

I tried.

It did not come easy.

Usually in times like that I pray for God to "receive" the person, for God to receive them with the same love and joy their family had for them. That's how I was trained to pray. But just because I was trained that way doesn't mean that's what I wanted to be praying. I really just wanted to pray him back. I wanted to pray the clock back a few hours so that right about then he'd be brushing his teeth or getting ready for bed or watching highlights from baseball's opening day. I wanted my prayers to make it so that I didn't have to be there, so that he didn't have to be there. And if I couldn't do that with my prayers, I wasn't sure God wanted to hear what it was I had to say. Because I didn't have any use for pieties. The only thing I wanted was to have him still with us.

Not until I was idling in my car years later, terrified for my own boy, who was Jackson's same age, did I understand how desperate that mother was to hear a reassuring word. I wanted someone to hand me a prayer like a blanket I could fold around my toes and pull up over my head to shut out the world. I sometimes say that, like doctors and nurses, I come home with blood on my clothes. I think holding Jackson, lifeless, in one arm and his mother, rigid in disbelief, in the other arm left me terrified of a similar scene playing out in our life. And so I didn't listen to Ali's not-so-cryptic concerns, and I ignored what I knew to be true somewhere in the back of my mind.

The shitty paradox about fear though is that avoidance of it makes it more likely you produce the very circumstances you wish to flee.

I gave Gabriel a hug in the school office. I signed the release form handed to me by the school social worker. Then we left for the same ER, the *same fucking room*, I'd driven to find Jackson ten years earlier.

"The county public school system protocol mandates that you take him to the ER for a mental-health evaluation," the social worker told me when I signed Gabriel's release.

Then she handed me a list of area hospitals and their addresses. I nodded. I held Gabriel's hand as we walked outside. He didn't push me away when I hugged him by the car, and he didn't let go. He held onto me and I onto him long enough for the first and second school bells to ring and fall silent. I squeezed him like the little boy in the Irving story, Tim, squeezes his bear as he ventures through the dark toward the dread looming for him.

I dreaded what I knew came next.

Having been a pastor for nearly twenty years, I was already familiar with the hospital's mental-health intake process. It's a heavy-handed, one-size-fits-all evaluation that, I suppose necessarily, feels criminal. Stopping home to pick up Ali, who'd rushed, frantic, from work, we drove together to the ER. At a red light, she texted me from the passenger seat: "I'm afraid we're going to lose control of what happens next to our son." I know in between I signed a patient registration form and filled out insurance information, but in my memory no sooner had we walked through the ambulance-bay doors than the male nurses had put what looked a prison uniform on Gabriel, tagged him, and carried him away from us, the fright we felt evident in his eyes.

"God dammit. He's never going to share his feelings and let people see another side of him ever again," I said to Ali.

"Look," she said, sniffing. She'd unzipped his backpack. His stuffed panda bear was inside, it's white mane nearly black from dirt he's had for so long.

"He must've grabbed it when we stopped to get you."

"He didn't think he was coming home again."

Judge Judy was playing on the TV on the ER waiting room wall.

Some domestic dispute. God, I'd never been so grateful for crap TV. I would've watched all the *Jerry Springer* and *Maury* and *Montel* you offered that day. Show me all the paternity tests, baby mommas, and petty lawsuits you can find—it felt great to know there was at least someone out there whose life was at least as upside-down shitty as our own in that moment.

"Maybe he has depression—maybe it's in his genes," I said, as we sat waiting, "I mean we don't know because he's adopted, maybe it's genetic."

She shot me her best *bless your heart (you idiot)* look. "Or maybe it's because his dad has incurable cancer and he's afraid you're going to die and kids are cruel and tease him about it."

"It could be that," I conceded sheepishly. "But suppose none of that had ever happened to us, the cancer, none of it, we might *still* be here. He might still be depressed. That's what makes people nervous about adopting, right? He's a mystery."

"I don't see what difference it makes," she said firmly, "when we're all a mystery, especially to ourselves as much as each other. We just have to love who we find as we find them."

I rested my head on her shoulder and asked her to put her arm around me.

I think I needed to become a pastor in order to be a Christian. The grammar of the faith comes hard to me. The daily dying of repentance and forgiveness comes harder still. It's like ripping off a Band-Aid every Sunday. I've got hairy ass arms. You wouldn't want to rip a Band-Aid off your arm if you didn't need to, would you? You wouldn't do it for *fun*. Fact is, I need my pension and dental tied to weekly appointments with the God who kills and makes alive. If I wasn't salaried by the sanctified I might not ever show up on Sunday.

Ali's different. Faith comes more naturally for her. Or rather, if faith is a gift from God, then faith comes to each of us from outside of us. Faith comes naturally to none of us, but Ali receives faith more bravely than me. Ali receives the gift with the same open arms she'd put around me.

In inverse proportion to my fear in engaging Gabriel's struggles, Ali displayed strength and poise (and angry mama-bear advocacy for our boy). To its degree, it was a side of her I'd not seen before. We all have shadow selves. Shadows need not be dark.

BANANA TRICK

"At first, I thought we were on the same page, but the self I brought to that page was a stranger to me."

I was confessing to Nancy, the counselor we'd started seeing, during a Thursday session. Gabriel had begun seeing her after I first got sick. Then, recently, not long after Gabriel's nightmare, Ali and I had started to talk with her too.

"Every time we stare into the mirror, we're looking at a stranger," Nancy replied. "We all have different selves, sides to us that surprise even us."

Like a splinter finally freed from your finger, her comment made me recall my grandpa. He had some secret selves of his own.

He died a few years ago. Specifically, I thought of a night when I was in the fifth or sixth grade. I was old enough to stay up later than my younger sister when we visited my grandparents' house. I'd stay up after everyone went to bed. With ninja-like quietness, acquired from having a mom who worked nights and slept during the day, I'd snuck into the kitchen. I raided the pantry and the fridge. Carrying a plate of sliced salami, pickles, chocolate, and cheese into the TV room, I turned the clock-like lever on their mammoth TV. I changed the channels, the tube booming dully with each click. Finding nothing but reruns of *Night Court*, I turned on their VCR. I saw there was already a tape inside it. I pressed play.

Someone who looked like Freddie Mercury from Queen was

doing something I'd never seen done before. Freddie was doing it to a blond woman with tight curls in her hair. Her hair *down there*.

I reached so fast for the VCR that I spilled my plate onto the floor. I hit the cabinet so hard that I spilled a half-empty glass of wine my grandpa had left on top of the TV cabinet. Burgundy bled all over the cream-colored carpet. But I didn't hit the stop button; instead I sat kneeling. Watching.

I let the stains seep into the carpet as I surreptitiously watched a few moments more. And then a few moments more. And then a few moments more. And then, the rest of it. Finally, I went through some of the drawers in the cabinet and found the case and a few others, hidden lazily underneath some investment journals and cattlemen magazines. The movie, which my grandpa had apparently been halfway through viewing, was titled *Pussy Talk*.

Adding the trappings of a plot device, the porno featured a talking—you get the picture. It was about as believable and sexy as a sock puppet. What was hard for me to picture, however, was how this stack of dirty movies squared with my portrait of my grandpa. Heretofore I'd only known him to watch, compulsively so, the stock market ticker tape on *CNBC* and the *PBS Newshour*. Then, reliably, he'd fall asleep on the sofa. Yet, suddenly *Pussy Talk* made sense of other parts to that portrait of my grandpa I'd previously only inchoately known. For example, my grandparents slept not just in different beds but in different bedrooms. They did so, I'd always believed (had I been told?), because my grandma snored too loud. The emotional distance between them though had often felt further than bedrooms on the opposite ends of the upstairs hallway. I'd never been able to put my finger on that dynamic. Then I watched Freddie Mercury put his finger . . . never mind. It's not as if pornography by itself indicates a marriage problem. And by then my grandma had long been exiled in a nursing home. With Alzheimer's, she'd already disappeared into the cloud of her own forgetting. So I don't begrudge my grandpa his jollies. But *Pussy Talk* in the absence of much obvious affection between my grandparents before she'd fallen ill, it revealed—or at least, implied—more than a few secrets. I pondered those secrets for over an hour as I worked furiously to expunge the blood-red evidence of my spill from the carpet.

The next morning I got in trouble for sneaking sips of his wine and spilling it on accident. I took the punishment. I never said a word about the movie. In fact, I had meticulously rewound it to the exact frame where it had been left.

After I watched it for a second time, that is.

We all have our secret selves.

I told Nancy about my grandpa.

Thinking about my grandma led me to tell Nancy about the guy I'd seen a few days earlier in line at the Safeway. Ali had texted me, asking me to stop on the way home and pick up a package of tampons. So naturally, I did what any mature, poised, self-confident man would do. I texted back: "Sure honey, no problem at all. Need anything else while I'm there?"

And then I drove to the grocery store, driving past the little Safeway just down the street, driving an extra eight miles, through two cellphone dead zones, waiting at four red lights, in order to get to the BIG SAFEWAY because the BIG SAFEWAY has SELF-CHECKOUT. What am I, an idiot? I'm not going to risk some checkout clerk announcing into that little microphone "We need a price check on tampons." Of course not; I've seen *Mr. Mom*. The self-checkout was designed for the express purpose of sparing husbands like me exactly that sort of shame.

Is it any coincidence that the increase in protected, safe-sex among young people coincides with the creation of self-checkout by Howard Schneider in 1992 for Price Chopper Supermarket in NYC? You think Magic Johnson made a difference in the fight against AIDS? He's got nothing on Howard Schneider whose invention gifted the world with a less awkward way to buy pro-phylactics.

So there I was at the BIG SAFEWAY, standing in the self-checkout queue, like a dutiful knight securing his queen what she requires, the feminine hygiene products discreetly hidden in my basket underneath a six-pack, the latest issue of *Garden and Gun*, and two bags of potato chips—I have cancer, why worry about my diet at this point?

Sure enough, as if to prove my hypothesis about Howard Schneider and the purpose of the self-checkout, I watched as the guy at the front of the line scanned and beeped from his basket the following items: one jar of kosher pickles, one bag of Flamin' Hot Cheetos, two(!) boxes of Trojans, one bottle of K-Y Warming Gel, and one package of Vermont Maple Syrup Breakfast Sausage Links.

"If you can do that after eating that more power to you," I said, not as quietly as I'd intended judging from the look he shot me.

As he did, the cart behind me hit me in the ankles for the third time. The cart belonged to that lady who dresses as Martha Washington at Mount Vernon near my house. I know it was her because she was dressed like Martha Washington, her hoop skirt that would make Sir Mix-A-Lot salivate knocking into the candy-bar rack. I turned around and glared at her again and then looked down into her cart. She had berries and sugar and flour and butter. *She's making a pie*, I thought to myself, *of course she's making a pie. What else would Martha Washington be doing besides white-washing indentured genocide?*

And then I noticed that underneath the berries and the flour and the sugar and the butter, Martha Washington was also buy-ing a copy of the *National Enquirer*. And *Star Magazine*.

Martha caught me looking into her cart, like a Peeping Tom.

"It's bad manners to be nosy."

"Lady, people who live in glass houses with slaves shouldn't throw stones."

"What?"

"Never mind."

The guy in front of me had started to scan and beep the items from his basket. He was wearing khakis and a distressed blue blazer. Standing out against his ruddy complexion was a neatly trimmed white beard. Sunglasses were perched on top of his curved orange Orvis cap, and his feet inside his boat shoes were bare. Basically he looked like someone who stills shells out money for Jimmy Buffett concerts.

He had a sticker stuck to the end of his finger.

It caught my eye, and I watched him. He pulled a package of steaks out of his basket, stuck the sticker over the one that was already on it, and scanned the steaks, a package of four.

Four dollars and change appeared on the screen.

Next, he took out a can of off-brand coffee, scanned it, and set it not in the bag but on top of the candy bars and instead from his basket he drew out a bottle of red wine and put it immediately, unscanned, into his shopping bag.

I looked over at the self-checkout clerk, who appeared to have the mental acuity of R. P. McMurphy at the end of *One Flew Over the Cuckoo's Nest*. He was oblivious; meanwhile, I was transfixed, staring like you do at a car accident or the Trump White House.

Next, he took out a package of shrimp, a couple of pounds it looked like, and he didn't scan it. He set it down it on the scale instead, and then he entered the code for bananas. He did that for a number of other items too—let's just say he bought a lot of bananas. Then he clicked "Finish and Pay."

And, as he pulled out his wallet, he looked sideways at me and he winked: "Surf and turf, for me and the wife."

"That's the most affordable surf and turf I've ever seen," I replied.

He shrugged his shoulders and gestured at the self-checkout machine: "If they're going to make me work at their store, then I deserve to get paid, right?"

And no joke, my first reaction, my immediate response was: "Huh, that's a good point."

I've no doubt I looked like an envious chump as I watched him walk away, none of us bystanders raising a finger or a decibel to stop him. As he walked away with his booty, the drowsy-looking self-checkout clerk suddenly sprang into action, bounding over to the shoplifter's register and grabbing the twenty dollars in change he'd left in the dispense tray. "Sir! Sir, you forgot your change!" he hollered, running after him through the automatic doors.

"What a motherfucker," Martha Washington muttered behind me.

"Manners," I said, shushing her.

Apparently using the code for bananas or a bunch of grapes and then socking a more expensive item of similar weight into your shopping bag—apparently that's a thing. It's such a thing, so common, the entire supermarket industry has a name for it: the Banana Trick. The industry has other names for other ways customers con the self-checkout. There's the "Pass-Around" and the "Switcheroo." According to the article "The Banana Trick: And Other Dark Arts of Self-Checkout Theft" in the *Atlantic Magazine*, beneath the bland veneer of your friendly neighborhood supermarket lurks something dark and ugly.[1]

It's you.

Most self-checkout shoplifters aren't thieves. Rather, without the threat of consequence, even the best of us do not reliably obey the oughts. The anonymity afforded by the self-checkout allows a shadow side of our true selves to reveal itself—a shadow side like, say, not uttering a word but instead admiring Jimmy Buffett's brass balls for turning a banana trick while the rest of us watched on like sheep.

"He got away scot-free?" Nancy the counselor asked.

1. Rene Chun, "The Banana Trick and Other Acts of Self-Checkout Thievery," *Atlantic Magazine*, March 2018.

I was alone in her office, an extra room on the third floor of an Episcopal Church. The names of former confirmands and their graduation dates were painted on the cinder block walls. Maps of mission trips long since taken covered some of the names and hung above stacks of bulk-ordered copies of the Book of Common Prayer. Gabriel was playing on my phone down the hallway. Ali called it an aftershock, a rupture that, if you traced it, would take you down to the earthquake day I was diagnosed. Cancer had exposed not just cracks and fissures in our marriage and in our family but in our selves too.

"I don't know that I like the me I've discovered that this has revealed. And if I don't like me . . ."

"That's the risk she took in marrying, right? That's the work of staying married," she replied. "You're actually saying 'I do' to a whole lot more people than what you can see or anticipate on the Big Day."

I nodded, hearing shades of my own advice to overconfident engaged couples in it.

"Really," she added, "we don't need to say 'I do' to the self we've fallen in love with. We need to make a vow to the self we do not yet see. That's the self that requires an unconditional promise from us because it might be a self that isn't all that loveable."

"I'm not so sure Ali likes the me she sees lately. Hell, I don't."

"Of course not," she kind of laughed, like she expected more from me as a professional courtesy. "People talk about their spouse as their better half, but that's nonsense. Your better half is the self you show to others, the false one that eventually, sooner or later, through some circumstance or another, your spouse gets wise to."

"I think I've discovered that I'm a good pastor to most everyone but the people in my family," I said, picking at a loose thread on the pillow in the rocking chair in which I sat.

Nancy's good, and I recognized her split-second decision to keep the silence, forcing me to make concrete my confession.

"I haven't engaged their grief, maybe because . . ."

"You're afraid of your own?"

I nodded and tried not to cry.

"What does that look like, not engaging their grief?"

"I'm a bad listener. I don't really empathize with them. I mean, I can't empathize when I'm avoiding their feelings altogether. I so wanted to get my life back; I just want to get on with my life. I guess I thought the sheer momentum of my gladness would drag them along, that if I was happy then they'd be happy, which only now strikes me as incredibly self-centered.

"And now *this* . . . *this* . . . to me, it feels like it's just erupted in our life, but I know the warning signs were all there and . . . I'm just ashamed to learn what a pussy I am.

"Sorry for my language," I said.

"Don't be."

"What I mean is, I'm ashamed to realize how timid I am. I was too afraid to pay attention, too afraid listen to Ali. Every time she tried to talk about it with me, I'd change the subject or make a joke instead. It's easier to crack jokes and slip between the eggshells with smiles."

"But that's the coward's way out—that's what you're saying about yourself, right?"

I nodded, surprised that hearing the bad news about us could simultaneously feel so good.

NO ONE IS PUNKING YOU

When you're the type of person who needs the every-Sunday deadline in order to be a Christian, you eventually learn the weird and naughty bits of the Bible that remain hidden to less frequent attenders. There's a trashy, cringe-worthy story in the Bible about an intense romance and an even more intense deception. I love to read it at weddings because I think it's the story of every romance that results in rings and vows. Leave it up to me and I'll choose 1 Corinthians 13, with its pablum about love being patient and kind, never out of ten times. Instead I'll choose the story of Jacob and Rachel (and Leah!) in Genesis.

Jacob is the grandson of Abraham. Despite being so faithful to God as to cut off the tip of his penis *as an adult*, Grandpa Abraham is a guy whose story is not exactly free from moral complexities. In a bind, Abraham passes his wife off as his sister and, later, pimps her out to Pharaoh. Rather than rehearse for you the entire book of Genesis, let's just say that Jacob is cut from the same cloth. On the run from his estranged brother, Jacob stumbles into love with a beautiful woman named Rachel. After negotiating a long engagement with Rachel's dad, Laban, there's a wedding. As at every wedding, there's a wild party. Jacob has a few drinks more than he should, and then has a few more. Then, drunk, Jacob stumbles into the honeymoon suite, a.k.a. the marital tent, just as he'd stumbled into love.

The morning after: Jacob rolls over in bed. Lying next to him is not Rachel but Laban's other daughter, Leah.

In the end, Jacob still gets Rachel, but in the process he gets a lot more than he bargained for: a second wife whom he doesn't find nearly as attractive or alluring. Later, God, in the dark of night and under the guise of a stranger, will change Jacob's name to Israel, and from him flow the Scripture stories that follow, including the Gospel stories.

Christ comes through Jacob and Leah, not Jacob and Rachel.

Jesus doesn't come through the beautiful Rachel who first enticed Jacob. The gospel is made flesh through Jacob's legacy with Leah, the one with "weak eyes," the one less lovely, maybe less loveable, and certainly the one harder for Jacob to love.

I use this story at weddings because, take away the animal husbandry and indentured servitude and patriarchy and polygamy, and it's the story of every marriage. The difference between happy marriages and the marriages that get torn asunder is that the former know Jacob's is the story of every marriage. So they don't freak out and leave when Jacob wakes up to Leah one day wondering where the hell Rachel went. This odd redneck story in the backwoods of Genesis is the story of every couple crazy enough to pledge "I do" to the stranger they love.

One day you wake up, and you expect to find Rachel, the person who made you say and do things you never thought you'd do or say, the person you dreamed dreams about and dreamed dreams with, and what do you find? Leah. Someone strangely unfamiliar. Someone who surprises you. Someone who shocks you, maybe even scares you. Someone who disappoints you.

But no one's punking you. The fact is that you married both of these people. You married their best self and their shadow side. You married the person who melts your heart and the person who has the power and maybe the proclivity to break it.

And they married you.

Jacob finding Leah when he expected Rachel is a reality that is inevitable in every marriage. All of us bring an unlovely, and maybe, to our mate, even unlovable, Leah to the marriage bed. Married or not, adults and kids, we're all simultaneously at once Rachel and Leah.

Give it time, your marriage will cast your shadow self out into the light. All the old arrangements of bed and board then will have to be rethought or thrown out altogether. Every relationship is fraught and folly because we never fully understand another person. Every person brings to the relationship both a lovely and loved "Rachel" as well as an unlovely and possibly unlovable "Leah."

Hell, marriage in the real world is more like Jacob waking up to find an orgy of unfamiliar Leahs snoring on the adjacent pillow. This is exactly why it doesn't matter whether men are from Mars or women are from Venus—because Jacob and Rachel both bring an entire constellation of other shadow selves they've snuck surreptitiously if unknowingly into their marriage.

The philosopher Alain de Botton says that expectations are the enemies of love. Born as they are by infatuation and passion, pop songs and princess weddings, expectations overlook one central fact about people in general: everyone has something substantially wrong with them once they become fully known.

This is why the marriage rite cares not at all why two lovers want to get married. It cares not a whit about their feelings for each other; it only wants to know what they propose to do about each other henceforth and when the shit hits the fan.

Despite our (not unreasonable) fears of the hospital psychiatrist admitting Gabriel to the mental-health unit for an indeterminate length of time, after a couple frantic and exhausting hours, we took Gabriel home. The psychiatrist concurred with our judgment that talking with his therapist was the best course of action. Ali made a low-key, normal-as-possible weekend for us. It was no easy feat. Every moment we were overcome with the urge to embrace one another, cling really, and reassure the other of our love.

"You can always talk to me," we must've offered every few minutes, as pathetic and desperate as the unwanted shrink from *Lethal Weapon*.

"There's no part of you that you need to hide from us," Ali told him over and over.

Come out, come out, come out, Leah, I legit prayed.

Every spouse soon enough knows what the church learned long ago. We remain, simultaneously so, Rachel and Leah. We are always the self we present and its shadow, which only one-way love can call forth into the light.

OPRAH IS THE BEST I CAN DO?

"I'm not argumentative," I shouted back at my laptop screen.

On Nancy's advice, I was taking the Enneagram personality assessment. According to Russ Hudson, who is the president of the Enneagram Institute, the Enneagram "is one of the world's most powerful and insightful tools for understanding ourselves and others. At its core, the Enneagram helps us see ourselves and others at a deeper, more objective level and be of invaluable assistance on our path to self-knowledge."[2]

On Nancy's orders, Gabriel was seeing her biweekly and, adding injury to my noninsured expense, I was paying to take a personality test to "find growth points in [my] marriage." Really, I was paying to meet my Leahs, whom Ali had already found in bed. After forking over $11.99 for the privilege of looking more deeply and objectively into my innards, I took the Russ Hudson Enneagram Type Indicator test (version 2.5), answering a series of binary questions such as:

Others should do:
  A) What's right
  B) What I tell them

Upon finishing, with the authority of the Sorting Hat at Hogwarts, the RHETI 2.5 told me that out of nine Enneagram types, I'm an 8.

"Why not a 9?"

I clicked open my report.

"The Challenger" it said at the top of my instantaneous report.

Okay, the Challenger, I thought to myself, I like the sound of the Challenger. According to the Enneagram Inventory, 8s are powerful (obviously), decisive (goes without saying), and self-confident (yep).

This is a good tool, I thought to myself, already starting to cut and paste it to send to Ali, my mother, and my high-school English teacher. Of course, I should've known that ever since Sally Ride "The Challenger" is something of a bad omen. I clicked the "Learn More" tab and the next page it called up communicated that as an 8 I'm also willful, confrontational, impatient, sarcastic, and argumentative.

"I am not argumentative. This test is stupid."

2. www.enneagraminstitute.com

It also said that, as an 8, I would tend to overestimate my emotional intelligence and empathy.

"Dammit," I whispered. I didn't send it to my mom or my high-school English teacher. I did show it to Ali though.

No doubt Russ Hudson would roll his eyes and say my response was predictable considering that 8s allegedly also believe they know better than everyone else, suspect they're always the smartest person in the room, and where you have opinions I have facts. After taking RHETI 2.5 five more times to the total tune of sixty dollars and rolling a hard 8 every time, I showed it to Ali, who read the rap sheet of an 8 and replied: "BAHAHAHAHAHAHAHA."

She actually snorted boogery ice-water out through her nose. Then she took the laptop from me and read aloud, as if for an audience: "Don't flatter an 8. It will only inflate their already large ego. When an 8 curses and uses inappropriate humor, just remember that's the way they are. An 8 doesn't mean to overwhelm you with bluntness, they just get restless when they perceive incompetence." Then she patted me on my sulking head and said "Don't you see honey, this is why so many people think you're an asshat."

Which is why I informed Ali I'd be giving her up for Lent and told her she can return to our bed sometime around Arbor Day. After taking the RHETI 2.5 six more times to no variance in results, I decided to email Russ Hudson and ask if I could get a refund from his fortune-cookie, tarot-card-reading racket. Ali kept me from clicking send.

I read a little more of my report, which told me that some of the other Enneagram 8s in history are Mahatma Gandhi, Albert Einstein, Abraham Lincoln, the guy from the Dos Equis commercials, and Jesus Christ. No. Just kidding. His report told me that among Enneagram 8s there are names like General George Patton, Richard Nixon, Saddam Hussein, Muammar Gaddafi, Donald Trump, and—I'm not joking—Oprah Winfrey.

"Really? Oprah is the best I can do? Well, at least Oprah isn't a despot or a dictator," I said to Ali after she stopped laughing at me.

"Really? She's not?"

Ali had already learned that she's a 6.

"I've always thought you were a 10," I winked at her.

Allegedly, as a 6, Ali's loyal and constant. And apparently she perceives uncertainty as a threat.

"So, having a husband with incurable cancer and a kid at the end of his wits about it must be a cakewalk," I said.

"I think it said I would thrive in just that situation," she said.

And then we both giggled.

More of Gabriel was stepping out of the shadows, in Nancy's office at least. Ali and I were discovering more of ourselves—or, more of our selves—which to my surprise left me feeling a different sort of envy for that banana-trick-turning Jimmy Buffett with the brass balls. At least he was a Rachel who knew one of his Leahs. Judging from the his-and-her portions of his looted bounty, his Jacob had already woken up to both of them.

The permutations of the Enneagram, all three-tiered variations within it, helped me to realize that, as Alain de Botton says, the difficulty we all have in our relationships is relationships *as such*. We see people all the time who have difficulty in their relationships, but we ignore it. We chalk the problem with those people up to *those particular people*. We think that we'll be different in our relationship. And we miss it: the problem with people's relationships is *relationships*. I think that's a good word because it's easy to think when things get hard that you've just placed your expectations on the wrong person, that you're in a relationship with the wrong person, when, really, *the problem in your relationship is relationships*.

With whomever you're married, by definition, you're married to more than one person. When you realize what the Bible realized on about page six, you realize how ludicrous it is to assume that the one to whom you've said "I do" will understand and empathize with you 100 percent of the time. The pop songs and princess weddings get love all wrong. The real heartache of love is not in finding someone but learning to tolerate the person you love once you've found them. The real heartache is learning to love the person with whom you fell in love because, in actuality, you've happened upon more than one person. It's not nothing that not even the storybooks end with "They lived happily—*always*—ever after."

It's no wonder, indeed it's inevitable, that conflict will occasion any and every conjugation of couples. The cast of characters called *you* is ever an unfolding mystery to your partner. But realizing that every Rachel brings a Leah to bed, that you're a loyal 6 and I'm an asshole 8, it changed how Ali and I conceived of conflict in our marriage. Suddenly, we could construe conflict as what happens when our love and marriage was working, not collapsing. Namely, conflict is what happens when love wins. Conflict means you've gotten to spy someone else across the full range of their life. Conflict means all their different selves have been revealed to you just as all of yours have been made vulnerable to them.

Jesus, as every football fan already knows in part, tells Nicodemus that to enter the kingdom we must be born again. And Jesus tells the disciples, who were busy elbowing past each other, that anyone who would enter his kingdom must become like children. If marriage is a sign and sacrament of the mystery of Christ's kingdom, then it follows that married people need to become like babies. And babies, as Saint Augustine notes, take time to realize that their mother is not just an extension of themselves. Little children take time to learn that their mother is someone else, a mystery to be discovered. Conflict and disappointment are, in fact, the fruits of the spirit of love, for it means you've done what Nicodemus couldn't do. In that you've gotten to know that the other whom you love is *other*; you've been born anew.

You've become like a child again.

Sitting around the fire pit laughing, we shouted for Gabriel to come outside. We had him take the Enneagram test. As it turned out, Gabriel's a 6 too.

"That's the same score I got!" Ali told him.

Even in the half light of the shadows spit against the wall of the shed from the fire pit, I could see the relief spill across his face.

"You're just as worried about your dad as I am!" Ali whispered into his ear. She'd already pulled him against her, hugging him, and in the shadows the fire flickered against the fence, I could see him smile.

CHAPTER 8.

PREMATURE EXONERATION

The End is music.

—Robert Jenson

APOCALYPSE CHOW

The psychiatrist at the hospital had given Gabriel his own sort of multiple choice test. One of the questions, we learned later:

How often do you think something terrible will happen?
A) Very often
B) Often
C) Sometimes
D) Never

He'd answered "A."

We needed a break from our house that often felt like a curio shop of cancer memories and suicide scares. Gabriel, we now knew, needed a respite. So we took a long getaway weekend at a friend's house in the mountains with my best friend Johanna and her husband Zack, Ali's brother Mike, and our friend Laura Paige.

Johanna had suggested we play *Cards against Humanity* after dinner. She moved the lit candlesticks to the center of the table and broke open the black box that came subtitled with the caveat "A party game for horrible people" while her son Zander and

Gabriel squawked and laughed downstairs in a game of their own.

Alexander sat on the other side of the open main floor, flipping TV channels. I watched as Alexander stopped on some religious channel where the televangelist Jim Bakker was hawking five-gallon buckets of freeze-dried food designed to survive the end-times for those waiting on the rapture.

"$135 for 154 meals! That's a good deal," Alexander muttered sarcastically.

"It's probably not a wise idea to take nutritional advice from a guy who did a four-year prison bid for fraud," I told him.

"Gross, it looks like papier mâché," he said.

"But look," I said, "the Peace of Mind Final Countdown Offer is 21,000 servings for only $4,500. You don't want Jesus to come back and be unhappy to see him because you're grumpy with the munchies, do you? Want to get left behind like a goat because you were having a sugar crash?"

Johanna rolled her eyes at our digression and, to explain the game to Ali and me, who were both new to it, Johanna read from the back of the box:

> Unlike most of the party games you've played before, *Cards against Humanity* is as despicable and awkward as you and your friends. The game is simple. Each round, one player asks a question from a black card, and the other players answer with their funniest white card.

The trick of the game, she explained, was being able to anticipate which card the person whose turn it was, the "Card Czar," would find the funniest. "It's like poker," she said, "but the whole point is knowing other people's tells." Sure enough, it was like *The Sting*; Ali was the Robert Redford across the card table from my Paul Newman, doing a dance no one else could see.

"I knew she'd choose bitches!" I delighted as I won the first round, correctly guessing which card Ali would choose.

Mike giggled and Alexander turned his head from the TV to

shake it at me, his stupid dad, as I raised my fists in victory like the runner in *Chariots of Fire*, bursting through the finish line, though I'm pretty sure if that pasty dude from *Chariots of Fire* refused to run on the sabbath, he wouldn't be playing a party game that came packaged, like *Girls Gone Wild* or *Hustler*, in an auspicious, nondescript black box.

"I knew she'd choose bitches!" I declared it again, reveling in this dirty Rorschach confirmation that I knew my bride right down to the vulgarities that would get her flushed but filled with glee.

"Well, duh?" Ali said. "It's obviously the funniest answer for 'Next from J. K. Rowling: Harry Potter and the Chamber of _____.'"

Harry Potter and the Chamber of Bitches.

"It's definitely funnier than *Chamber of Ebola*," I pointed out, citing one of the limp possibilities someone around the table had offered. "*Chamber of Bitches* could be a movie about a whole bunch of Hermione clones," I laughed.

"I like Hermione," Alexander said absent-mindedly, his face glued to the TV, "She's hot."

I'd run the table, knowing exactly which card Ali would choose every time.

Groans occasioned our giggles every turn.

If the average, everyday arguments weren't evidence that the full range of our selves have been laid bare to one another, over seventeen married years, then our ability to kick ass at *Cards against Humanity* sure was. We dominated, not only because we've been friends since we were fifteen and, in love, have pored over the details of one another like an artist over a master's canvas, but also because we've fought like hell, can drive each other batshit crazy, and are each the chief neighbor the other fails to love as much as self. We were the other's only competition in the game because both us have been for the other what the marriage rite in the Book of Common Prayer calls "a counselor in perplexity"; that is, we'd both been perplexed yet passionate beholders of the strange mystery of the other.

My best friend Johanna, delighting that this game was her idea, guffawed until she dry heaved. Her husband, Zack, smiled, poured himself a whiskey, and reshuffled the cards for another game. Mike put his iPhone into an empty glass hoping the emptiness of it would amplify the music it played. My friend Laura Paige sat next to him and, deadpan, said to her own whiskey glass: "I still think 'Harry Potter and the Chamber of Ebola' is funny."

Mike giggled at Laura Paige. My one and only matchmaking success—the two of them are married now. Some time that night, during this game, maybe because of the playful vulnerability of it, they crept, on tiptoes, into courtship. Or, as an Enneagram 8, I just like to think I'm responsible for their relationship.

It's not just your different selves that marriage brings into your marriage. Marriage also brings into your life friendships you would not have had were it not for marriage. Marriage brings into your life friendships that depend upon your marriage and would suffer should your marriage end just as your marriage surely depends on them. Just as following Jesus requires a congregation to hold the baptized accountable to cross-bearing, so too do a couple's vows of trust, intimacy, and fidelity—forever, in sickness and in health—require a congregation called friends to accompany them in their faithfulness. It's why, for instance, I refuse to preside over private weddings. Whether the bride and groom are religious or not, sooner or later they're going to need some kind of congregation.

Ali and I needed them to stay together, in love, for our own sake. These were the friends that had sustained us when we most needed it, and them coming to our rescue begat other betrothals. Had Mike not moved in with us when I first got sick to help take care of me, he and Laura Paige would not be married now.

Playing *Cards against Humanity* and watching Ali watch me,

knowing how I'd respond to each move she made, the *I love you* in her eyes, it reminded me of our first time. Like our first kiss (at a high school dance to U2's "With or Without You" [cliché I know]), it was her initiative because I'm fundamentally a coward but was especially terrified by the tall leaps and bounds to which she was out of my league. Teenagers, we'd been watching a movie at my house in the room over the garage. Well, not really watching it—more like the movie was the soundtrack for our own, a pastiche of remembered scenes from *Weird Science*. While we were making out, my mom had started to fight with my dad on the phone. About child support, I think. Embarrassed, I suggested we go outside to spend the time we had left before her curfew was due.

We were in the garden. The moon was full and so were her lips. I sat down on the wood of a raised flower bed and she sat on my lap facing me, her sundress splayed over me, one of the straps fallen down from her shoulder. My hands ran up her thighs to the lace edges of where they'd never ventured before. In the full moon, I could see her staring at me, grinning, seeing me in all my need to hear it said and all my frightened impotence to say it myself.

"I love you," she said, kissing me with an urgent permanence I'd not felt before. There in the garden, my sandals slipped off my feet and my toes scrunching the soft, black topsoil with her every kiss, we weren't naked but we were as unashamed as Eve and Adam, creatures content—maybe for the first time—with our creatureliness. "I love you too," I said into her chest, my heart beating in my throat. I wonder if we experience the later days of our relationships as less intense because we seldom make ourselves as vulnerable as we do when we give or receive that first *I love you*.

And it occurred to me that night playing *Cards against Humanity*, though I didn't say it out loud, that if the world was about to end and Christ's triumphant arrival was imminent, then this silly, horrible game shared by friends and lovers unabashedly revealing their vulgar, naughty sides to one another was a more faithful way to welcome the Lord than a flood bucket full of freeze-dried food.

Say what you will about the bawdy party game, that night sharing whiskey and obscenities around the candlelit table we were free; meanwhile, the huckster preacher on the TV was peddling the opposite of freedom. He was selling fear.

GOD DOESN'T GIVE A DAMN

Jackson, the little boy about Gabriel's age who hung himself years ago in his closet filled with Lego and action figures, died a few days before Harold Camping, another huckster preacher, predicted on his radio broadcasts that the world would end, in judgment and fury, on the twenty-first of May.

I'd gone into town to purchase a black tie to wear to Jackson's grave. I was in a hurry, still feeling numb from feeling him in my arms. But standing there on the corner, blocking my path, were four or five men and women, evangelists. A couple of them of were holding foam-board signs high above their heads. The signs were brightly illustrated with graphic images of a lake of fire, a seven-headed dragon, and a terrible-looking lion with scars on its paws. At the bottom of one of the signs was an illustration of people, men and women—and fucking children—looking terrified, looking like they were weeping.

A couple of them were passing out pamphlets. I tried to slip by unnoticed into the Banana Republic on the corner. One of them tried to hand me a tract, so I just held up my hands and said, "I'm Buddhist."

But the young man blocking my path wasn't fooled. He pointed at my open collar and said: "But you're wearing a cross around your neck."

"Oh that," I said in mock surprise.

The young man looked to be in his twenties. He didn't look

very different from the models in the store window next to us. He handed me a slick, trifold tract, gave me a syrupy smile, and said, "Did you know Jesus Christ is coming back to Earth on May 21 to judge sinners into everlasting torment?"

Then he started talking about the end of the world. I flipped through his brochure; it was filled with images and Scripture citations from Revelation.

"Martin Luther said Revelation was a dangerous book in the hands of idiots," I mumbled.

"What's that?" he asked.

"Oh nothing, just thinking out loud."

Then he asked me if I was saved.

"Because," he said, "Jesus Christ is returning May 21 to destroy this sinful world, but Jesus will forgive and spare the tribulation all those who invite him into their hearts."

Now, don't get me wrong, I'll be the first to admit it. Sometimes, I'm prone to sarcasm. Sometimes, as the geezers in my church like to point out, I have a tendency to be abrasive. But that Friday, the day after Jackson, what I felt rising in me was more like anger.

"Lemme ask you something," I said, "since you seem to know your Bible."

The evangelist smiled and nodded. He looked electrified to be, all of a sudden, useful.

"Doesn't the Bible call Jesus the Lamb of God who takes away the sins of the whole world?" I asked, feigning naïveté.

He nodded a sanctimonious grin.

"Well then, which ones did he miss?"

He furrowed his brow, confused, as shoppers pushed past us to get to the bus stop.

"Sins, which sins did he miss?" I'd raised my voice now, my pretense falling away and my righteous anger welling up in the teardrops threatening at the corner of my eyes. "Did Jesus take away all the sins of the world, or did he only get some of them?"

No sooner had he started to mouth the word "all" than I was back on him and down his throat.

"Really?! Because from your signs and pamphlets, it sure as hell looks like Jesus missed a whole lot of sins, that he's got a whole lot more to do in the judgment-for-sins department."

He started to give me a patronizing chuckle, so I pressed him. "And, wait a minute, didn't Jesus say, whilst dying for the sins of the *whole* world, 'It is finished?' Isn't that, like, red-letter?"

He nodded and looked over my head to his supervisor behind me. I was shouting now.

"And doesn't it say, too, that in Jesus God has chosen us from *before* the foundation of the world?"

"I think so," he said. "I'm not sure."

"Well, damn straight it does," I hollered. "Ephesians, and, looking at you all with your bullhorns and pictures of dragons and judgment, I'm just wondering how, if God's chosen us all in Christ from before the beginning of *everything*, you think any of us with our puny, pathetic, run-of-the-mill sins—which have all been taken away already—can gum up God's plan?"

Okay, so maybe I was feeling a little sarcastic.

"I'm not sure you understand how serious this is, sir," he said to me.

"Oh, I got it, all right. I just think it's you who doesn't take it seriously, not enough apparently to take Jesus at his word. When it comes to our sins, God literally doesn't give a damn anymore."

It was right about then I became aware that I was creating a scene. A small crowd had stopped and were watching us trying to determine if this was intentional street theater. And I could tell from the look on his face that this evangelist was now much less concerned about my eternal salvation, and if he could he'd probably volunteer to throw me in the lake of fire himself.

He reached into his back pocket and pulled out a glossy business card.

"Maybe you should talk to a pastor instead," he said.

"Yeah I'll think about it," I said, and I walked inside the store to buy a necktie I could wear beside a four-foot coffin, thinking how silly it is we worry about avoiding loud colors for such occasions. Nothing, after all, is as garish as declaring, "earth to earth, ashes to ashes" above a little boy's open grave. I tore off the tie and threw it into a trashcan at Arlington National Cemetery right after I buried Jackson in a plot underneath an old gnarled tree where his four-star grandfather will one day be laid to rest.

It wasn't until we had our own suicide scare with Gabriel, thinking of needing to buy another black tie and bearing our own boy's body in a short casket, that my own death seemed a small worry to me. And to Ali.

Normally I hate pastors who quote C. S. Lewis, so forgive me. Lewis said that lovers gaze at each other, but friends—married friends—stand beside each other, shoulder to shoulder, looking at a common vision.

Or a shared struggle.

With Gabriel's scare, we'd been given a different diagnosis with which to deal.

When Ali and I began the adoption process for Gabriel, we had to answer a battery of questions and go through several interviews assessing the health of our relationship, the depth of our faith, and the strength of our self-image. The adoption agency wanted to verify that we weren't adopting a child because we needed to have a child to make us happy. I often wish biological parents had to go through the same process. Heard the wrong way, this can sound harsh, but it's true: from "I do" all the way unto death, your primary commitment is to your spouse, not your kids. When God lamented Adam's loneliness in the garden, God didn't give Adam a child. God gave Adam a spouse. The only person to whom you'll ever swear vows is your spouse, not your kids.

"You can't cultivate a marriage or even survive one by loving your kids," I always tell prospective brides and grooms.

"However, you can raise loved, loving children by making a loving marriage your priority. Marriage is about the person you're married to. It's got to be. If nothing else, do it for the kids." It's good advice. Had Ali and I not heeded it ourselves, I don't think we would have had the resources to face the fright Gabriel had given us. Because we'd made our marriage a priority, we could now stand shoulder to shoulder and make him our priority.

If my death was no longer something to be feared, then my reprieve from it and my *miracle marriage* suddenly were freed from any burden of earning or expectation. While I still hope my past doesn't yet outweigh my future, I'm free to let my present play itself out as gift rather than gauntlet.

We've never been happier.

SHOULDER TO SHOULDER

The scare Gabriel had given us shook me awake. Suddenly I realized that I really do believe every word I hollered at those street preachers. Who knows, maybe I believed it then, too, at that street corner on the eve of the "end of the world." Now I so believe it I'm willing to stake my death on it. I'm willing to live out my remainder tethered only to it.

Despite the ubiquity of doomsday hucksters and pulpy *Left Behind* movies, if the gospel is true and the cross is to be trusted as a complete and finished work, then the same refrain that announces the beginning of the work of God in Jesus Christ occasions the conclusion of it too, as well as our place in it: "Do not fear." The headline the angel Gabriel gives to the gospel abides to its very end. The end is not the stuff of scary signs and bullhorns bludgeoning passersby with a message about a monster god. Death need not be feared—no matter the nature of the life that preceded it—because the good news of the gospel is that the character of my life or your life is not the good news. The god who dies in Christ's grave never to return is the angry god conjured by our angry hearts and anxious imaginations. If it's the devil in the desert who speaks in if/then conditions, then the devil's chief work in the world is to convince us that our sins are more consequential than Christ's complete and total triumph over them.

Speaking just from the mission field of my own marriage, I can testify that most of the damage I do to myself and to others isn't because I'm convinced God doesn't condemn me for my sins but because I fear—despite my faith—the judgment I think I deserve. And so I do damage, making others the object of my anxious attempts to make myself look better and be better than I really am. I think this explains why the people against whom we sin the most are the people we love the most. They're the ones who've invested the most in us and we in them; consequently, we want to impress them the most and, as a result, they become the ones against whom we most sin. But no spouse deserves to be the occasion of their lover's project of self-justification; what's more, no spouse can endure the burden of such an expectation.

The hilarity of the gospel, though, is that, in the foolish economy of God's love, all your sins are free, putting us back in the same position as Eve and Adam before there was a single sin, without any reason for shame or blame, with no need to hide from one another, free to be seen and to be known, content to be creatures, free to be with and for one another in all our dirty detail.

PALLIATIVE CARE FOR THE DEAD IN CHRIST

After we returned home from the long weekend, I went to the hospital for another of my quarterly CT scans to insure the monthly maintenance chemo was keeping the cancer at bay down deep in my bone marrow. I stripped into a gown and put my clothes in a locker, and the nurse led me into a tiny prep room.

"Grab a seat," she said pointing to a beige recliner.

She rolled the tray with her syringe on it toward me and, rolling her fingers along my forearm, looked for a vein.

"In case you're interested," she said, "here's your report from your last scan. You probably already have a copy."

I squinted in a short, secret grimace as she stuck me. The contrast started to course into me as I stared at the positronic image of me from my last visit. Without skin or bones in it, I looked like man-shaped jellyfish.

"At least my man-parts look ample in the picture," I mumbled.

She laughed as she taped the syringe into place.

"If you've got to pay huge medical bills, I guess it should be at least one perk," I said.

"The CT camera enlarges things," she said.

"My wife tell you that?" I started to ask, but her deadpan face had already broken into a smile.

All it takes is a snapshot of your insides to see yourself as something fearfully and wonderfully *made*, a creature as any other that God, like a taxidermist, has stuffed with life for a time.

"It'll be about twenty minutes or so for the contrast. You okay?" she asked, about to leave.

Prior to previous scans, I'd had small panic attacks sitting there in the tiny prep room thinking about my life in terms of the odds and averages and wondering when the house was going to win.

"Yep," I said, "I'm fine."

And here's the thing: for the first time, I really was fine.

"What's the worst that could happen?" I said as she walked out. I wasn't being sarcastic.

Down in the bowels of the hospital, I couldn't get a signal on my phone, so, with my free arm, I rummaged through the cache of books and magazines attached to the recliner.

Shoved in between past issues of *People* and *Vanity Fair*, I pulled out an old *New York Times*. I smoothed it out on my lap on top of the picture of man-shaped-jellyfish-me, and I read a story about a man named B. J. Miller, a palliative care doctor at a facility called Zen Hospice in San Francisco.

One Monday night when B. J. Miller was a sophomore at Princeton University, he and two friends went out drinking. Late that night, on their way back, drunk and hungry, they headed to the convenience store for sandwiches. A commuter train was parked at the rail junction near the convenience store there that night, idle, tempting Miller and his friends to climb up it. Miller scaled it first. When he got to the top, eleven thousand volts shot out of a piece of equipment and into Miller's watch on his left arm and down his legs. When his friends got to him, smoke was rising from his shoes. B. J. Miller woke up several days later in the burn unit at St. Barnabas Medical Center to discover it wasn't a terrible dream. More terribly, he found that his arm and his legs had been amputated. Turmoil and anguish naturally followed those first hazy days, but eventually Miller returned to Princeton where he ended up majoring in art history. The broken arms and ears and noses of ancient sculptures helped him affirm his own broken body as beautiful.

From Princeton, Miller went to medical school, where he felt drawn to palliative care because, as he says: "Parts of me died early on. And that's something, one way or another, we can all say. I got to redesign my life around my death, and I can tell you it has been a liberation. I wanted to help people realize the shock of beauty or meaning in the life that proceeds one kind of death and precedes another."[1]

After medical school, Miller found his way to Zen Hospice in California, where their goal is to de-pathologize death; that is, to recover death as a human experience and not a medical one. They impose neither medicine nor meaning onto the dying. Rather, as Miller puts it, they let their patients "play themselves

---

1. Jon Mooallem, "One Man's Quest to Change the Way We Die," *New York Times*, January 8, 2017, 39.

out." Whoever they've been in life is who they're encouraged to be in their dying.

For example, the *New York Times* story documents how Miller helped a young man named Randy Sloan, who was dying quickly of cancer, die doing what he loved to do: drinking Bud Light and playing video games. Talking about Sloan's mundane manner of dying, Miller said: "The mission of Zen Hospice *is* about wresting death from the one-size-fits-all approach of hospitals, but it's also about puncturing a competing impulse: our need for death to be a transcendent experience."[2]

According to Miller, most people aren't having profound, super-spiritual, or transformative moments in their deaths, and if you hold that out as an expectation, they're just going to feel like they're failing. They're going to feel like there is something they must be doing that they're not doing. They're going to worry that they're doing something wrong, or they're going to fear that they're not doing enough. Miller instead frees his patients from "the crushing weight of unhelpful expectations."

What's miraculous, B. J. Miller contends, more miraculous than empty, contrived spiritual gestures, is watching what the dying do with their lives once they learn they have the freedom not to do anything.

We die the way we live.

Just as many die thinking that there's something more spiritual or profound or meaningful they should be doing and worrying that they aren't doing it or aren't doing it right or doing it enough, as a pastor I've learned that most people, religious or not, live with that same anxiety: "What am I supposed to be doing?"

And nowhere more so than in marriage.

What should I be doing as a husband? What should I be doing as a wife?

2. Mooallem, "One Man's Quest," 39.

It gets even more burdensome when you freight it with the modifier Christian.

What should I be doing as a Christian husband? As a Christian wife? What should our Christian marriage do and be?

Maybe it takes an amputee agnostic working at a crunchy Buddhist hospice on the Left Coast to point it out: Miller's is the work of the gospel too—to unburden you from the crushing weight of expectations.

The gospel is that you are saved by God's grace alone and that it is yours simply by trusting it. The gospel is like palliative medicine for the dead in Christ. The gospel is that you are forgiven and justified and loved exactly as you are. Full stop.

And so is your spouse.

The work of the gospel is to unburden you from trucking the crushing weight of that question into any part of your life or your death but especially into your marriage: "What must my marriage be doing to please God?" The gospel, as Gerhard Forde says in *Where God Meets Man*, unburdens you to ask a different question, a question that leads to something more miraculous and even more beautiful: What do you want to do with your marriage now that you have the freedom not to do anything with it?

DUST JACKETS

Many engaged couples I meet have only vague goals for their marriage: *We want to be happy. We want to have a family. We want to be best friends.*

"That's all well and good," I've typically told them, "but how in the hell do you measure goals that airy?"

Likewise, I've met with many married couples who describe their marriage as "stagnant" or "stuck." They have no idea where they're trying to go.

"You only put your car in drive to head toward a destination," I tell them, feigning a fraudulent wisdom. "Otherwise you leave it in park. Or neutral. And if you're not headed to any particular, specific destination, it's not long before you're wondering why you're wasting your time sitting in a car that's not moving. And it's not long before you get annoyed with all the commotion the kids are making in the back seat."

Theologians use the term *telos* to describe human life. It's Greek for *end*. By it, they mean that having been made in God's image, a life well-lived is one with a trajectory that points to and proceeds toward Christ and his grace. Sin is literally something that gets our lives off track.

Husbands and wives should have specific, concrete goals for their marriage. Not only should couples have micro goals for each stage of their marriage, they should have macro goals for their marriage as a whole. It's just common sense. If you don't know where you're going, you can end up anywhere but there. And if you don't know where you're trying to get, it's very easy to get hung up on things that don't matter and to compromise on things that do.

For years I've told engaged couples to imagine their married life as a story or memoir—as a book. "What do you want the dust jacket to say?" I ask them. "What do you want the summary of your story together to be?"

And I tell them to be damn specific. I tell them I don't want to hear something like "Dick and Jane were just so happy together because they loved each other so much." That's usually what their first drafts will say. I tell them they should choose, together, three to five things they want to accomplish in their marriage and weave that into dust-jacket summary:

Dick and Jane built their dream house at X.

Dick and Jane traveled to Y.

Dick and Jane worked to make sure their relationship was always characterized by Z, that nothing ever changed _____ about them.

Sure those three to five things can change as life happens and things change, but you've got to be intentional about identifying what the new three to five things are when that happens. You've got to be intentional about what the rewrite on the dust jacket says now.

"This isn't about married people having a bucket list," I counsel them, "It's about married people having a compass to steer by. You have to have an agreed-upon basis by which you'll make decisions and set priorities as a couple. You have to be able to say as a married couple: *These are the three to five things we refuse to compromise on in our marriage.* Because the truth is, if you have goals in your marriage you won't compromise on, it's less likely that other things will compromise your marriage. You've got to know the ending of the story you're trying to get to. You've got to know what your dust jacket says."

I think it's good counsel for couples, and it's always been received as such, but I don't think I ever appreciated how the oughts accuse us as couples into thinking our story needs to be about something awesome and extraordinary. With the dust-jacket lingo, I gave couples a good image by which to think about the trajectory of their marriage.

I just never gave them enough freedom.

I didn't convey clearly to them: What do you want the dust jacket of your story to say now that you have the freedom for it not to say anything in particular at all?

When the Peasants' Revolt roiled the kingdoms of sixteenth-century Germany, the unprecedented violence and depravity of war spurred a wave of doomsday preaching and end-times predictions. Many churchmen, including Martin Luther, suspected the apocalypse was near and Christ's return was around the corner. With the world upside-down and maybe nearing closing time, Luther didn't put on a sandwich board or pick up a bullhorn. He didn't throw himself into prayer or fasting. He didn't become a prepper, packing away food into flood buckets.

He got married.

If the end was nigh and Christ was near, Luther didn't think he was required to be found doing super-spiritual, pious, religious acts, as though he needed to impress God or had any outstanding IOUs. No, if the Maker of heaven and earth was about to bring heaven to earth, then Luther wanted to be found by the Creator living as a creature. He wanted to be found tending his little patch of the garden of God, an unanxious Adam with an at-ease Eve, both of them unafraid because of the happy news that the Creator has already borne all the brokenness of the Old Creation away in his body and has returned to still the groanings and labor pains of a New Creation awaiting its promised full and final redemption.

Marriage, therefore, isn't a religious vocation.

It is a creaturely one.

Marriage is one of the ways we give flesh-and-blood expression to the gospel announcement that "religion" (what we do to get right with God) is over and done, consummated once for all by the Bridegroom, Jesus Christ. Marriage is a means that two creatures, in all their sin and infuriating imperfections, wonder and beauty, embody the hilarious news of God's grace.

Marriage is a creaturely vocation because the work of religion is finished for all time. In marriage, we can enter one another's lives fully, embracing another as they are and accepting the two of you together as you are, with all your dirt and in all your delight, freed by the knowledge that, because Christ has taken care of everything, your marriage doesn't *need* to be anything.

Your marriage doesn't need to be anything other than what you want it to be.

An ordinary marriage can become something extraordinary, a sacrament even, once it's freed from the burden of being a religious undertaking.

It's true, as I said at the outset, that by their mutual vows husband and wife become a parable of the love of God. But that's not as weighty or freighted as it sounds, for the Christ who compares his kingdom to a wedding party also compares his kingdom to a stupid sheep who can't help but get itself lost.

By themselves, sheep are lunch for wolves. Not only are sheep weak and stubborn and easily led astray, they're completely useless. Sheep aren't like other animals. Sheep aren't like asses. Sheep don't do any work by which they merit their worth. Even goats do work by which they earn their value. The only real work—if you can call it work—a sheep performs is trusting the shepherd's voice.

By our daily "I do's" to one another, living in sin yet loving one another in spite of those sins, we become a parable of the Shepherd who found us lost. He put us on his shoulders and carried us back once and for all, so that, as his friends, we can rejoice in one another as the stupid but spectacular creatures we are.

WHAT WILL GET LOST HAS ALREADY BEEN FOUND

After our long weekend away, our family started binge-watching the SYFY remake of the series *Battlestar Galactica*. It's Ali's favorite show, and we judged the boys finally old enough to appreciate the philosophical themes while still squinting on our orders through the sexual content. Ali loves the show for its main character, the heroine Starbuck, a brash, foul-mouthed, hard-drinking, but courageous and selfless space pilot who upsets all the gendered conventions of adventure stories.

One school night we were all sitting at the dining-room table for supper. The boys were picking at the bits of faded red onion and wilted mint in the orecchiette and sausage I had made for them.

"Can we watch *Battlestar Galactica* while we eat dinner?" Alexander asked.

"Absolutely not," I said. "Eat your dinner."

"Come on, why not?" Alexander asked.

"Because that's not what families do. Families eat together at the dinner table and talk about their day and enjoy each other's company," I'd raised my voice, and now I was shoveling food joylessly into my mouth.

"But we talk about our day more and enjoy each other's company more while we're watching *Battlestar Galactica*," Alexander observed.

"Right? Now we're just listening to each other chew," Gabriel muttered.

"Well, why do we have to do what other families do?" Ali said to me, glancing down, her crack of a smile reflecting in her plate.

"What?" I asked, genuinely surprised as my whole domestic-dad performance was contrived for her sake.

"Who cares what other families do? Why do we need to worry about that?" she said as the boys stared at the miracle being birthed before them.

"But . . . but . . . but," I came up empty.

"We do have fun watching *Battlestar Galactica*, and we do chat about our day while we watch it. Why do we have to eat here at the table and pretend we'd rather do this than watch it? Why aren't we free to do what we want?"

"Because . . . I don't know. I mean, if it's okay with you then I guess . . . sure." I said.

"Yes!" Gabriel thrust his chair out so quickly it tipped over and fell against the floor.

"Just don't get food on my sofas!" Ali ordered, but she was smiling so they knew that even that would be forgiven.

Alexander was still watching us, still looking at me, to make sure it wasn't a trap.

"Go on, she's the boss," I said, giving her a playful, sloppy kiss as I stood up.

Married friends may stand shoulder to shoulder against a shared struggle, but marriage is not like a military parade. Marriage, Robert Capon notes in *Bed and Board*, is more like a dance where one leads and the other follows, an inequality of role not merit. And, as time goes on and the music of your life together changes, the roles will shift, and the other will take the lead. Marriage is not a march where you're both doing the same thing, shoulder to shoulder, or one behind the other.

Marriage is a dance. It's close up, often aggravatingly so. It's face to face. It's a tango of loving and being loved. Of initiating and responding. Of repenting and forgiving. Of showing patience and showing gratitude for patience. It's a movement of actions to which your feelings are often incidental. Marriage is a dance where the work is learning when to lead and when to respond. It's exhausting and hard and beautiful and fun, and it takes practice. Marriage is a dance where two equals take on different and unequal but fluid roles in order that both may contribute to the perfection of the whole: the particular parable, that is every parable, of your life together.

The dance two do with their lives lived together, it's meant to be a live performance, a spontaneous street-theater parable of how God in Christ loves us all. The vows by which bride and groom bind themselves to one another are outrageous promises to make to any sinner, most especially to the one whose dirty underwear you'll see on the bathroom floor for several decades. It's a difficult dance, marriage. But it's not the high-stakes burden it sounds like. It's not like *America's Got Talent* or *Dancing with the Stars*. There are no losers.

No one is voting you to go home, because by God's one-way love called grace you're already home free. With Jesus, what will get lost has already been found. In other words, you are free to dance with your partner knowing that every misstep is already forgiven. As far as the judging of your dance goes, Christ has already said all of that's finished with, with perfect scores for everyone.

The music of his party already kicked on in a garden near a cross on a hill, and the needle will never reach the end of the record. It's a hard and difficult dance to do, but there are no stakes, no penalties to messing it up. As the prodigal's elder brother can tell you, the only way you fail at this dance is by being a begrudging wallflower and refusing to join in the Bridegroom's party.

THE END IS MUSIC

The last black card we played for *Cards against Humanity* that long weekend away prompted us with: "This is the way the world ends. This is the way the world ends. Not with a bang but with _____."

The whiskey glasses were empty and our heads were tipsy and the candles were burnt down to nubs. Gabriel had gone up to bed, smiling a goofy grin in his sleepiness; if only for a while he was just a boy again. Alexander had fallen asleep on the floor, flipping channels, one TV huckster preacher turned into another, different faces but the same fear.

Ali was again the card czar. It was her turn to choose. She turned over the possibilities we'd tossed onto the table. I looked at the answers the others had offered ("Tasteful Sideboob," "Cuddling," "Letting Everyone Down").

And I knew she'd choose mine: "Neil Patrick Harris."

This is the way the world ends. This is the way the world ends. Not with a bang but with Neil Patrick Harris.

Ali doubled-over, giggling, and couldn't stop.

"It doesn't really make sense, but . . . Neil Patrick Harris just makes it funny," Ali said, pulling my card toward her with her long, thin index finger as her knowing eyes locked onto mine.

I could've played the other card I still had in my hand. It would've fit better, and it would've been perfect in a way, not to mention true. It read: "God." *This is the way the world ends. This is the way the world ends. Not with a bang but with God.*

For my money, I bet it ends with music.

I like to think the music for Ali and me is that John Prine song about a wife at her wits' end and an unimpressive, exasperating husband reaching their rainbow in spite of themselves and, by sheer grace or dumb luck, discovering that they are, the two of them together, "the big door prize."

And they have been all along.

Ali will tell you: it's our song.

The end of everything is God, sure enough. But the God who shows us his ass rather than his glory, who kills with words, and who hides behind suffering is a God whose end just might surprise us and sound like a corny country song about sinners sitting on a rainbow that they manifestly do not deserve.

In the meantime, I can't predict what's in store for us.

The house always wins. Sooner or later, the floor boss will come tell me I'm longer comped my stay here. I'll lose this hand I've been dealt. But I do not fear what I believe another has paid for me, gratis. I fear what the wages of my end will mean for Ali and the boys, but I do not fear the end.

I worry now as a father, but Ali and I are free of the burden of needing our marriage to merit the temporary miracle we've been given. It's not like make-up sex all the time, and it doesn't have to be (nor, at forty, could I muster that much energy). In the process, we've realized just how, as a miracle, my temporary one doesn't much measure up to the miracle that we found each other in the first place. And both miracles pale in comparison to the miracle that we're learning, in fits and starts, to tolerate the person we've found and love.

The house always wins, but it's sure as hell fun to play while you can. So why not play with the piled-high stack of free grace you've been given and stop worrying when your dice will run cold?

Ali and I are free now from the accusing oughts we felt in the days and months after my reprieve from death. We're free to love one another in marriage and mess up along the way because, unlike the *Bachelor*, we both believe the Bridegroom has already given us the rose for his wedding feast from before the very foundation of everything. He has already outfitted us for it with the garment bestowed on us in our baptisms. So, we're free to love and live, awaiting the end, unafraid.

We can spite the noses right off of our faces in stubborn love, but nothing we do to one another can frustrate forever the stubborn love of God who is the end to every one of our silly, sinfilled, choose-your-own-adventure stories.

Only a God whose glory is shame and whose grace often looks like the belly of a whale could appreciate the irony:

The trick to making marriage work between "I do" and death is trusting the good news that there is no *work* your marriage needs to do.

The hilarious good news of grace means your marriage is free to be whatever you want it to be. Your marriage is even free to fall short of what you wish for it.

Knowing we're free to fail has made our marriage more successful than it's ever been.

Whenever it comes for me, it's true. *This is the way the world ends. This is the way the world ends. Not with a bang but with God.*

But I didn't play the card.

It would've been too serious. Ali would've rolled her eyes at the earnestness of it and not picked it exactly because she would've known it was my card.

I didn't lay it on the table but, turning off the lights and turning down the bed, "God" was soon on both of our lips, his name taken not in vain, sacred not profane, for on the free lips of every married lover it is the very groaning and moaning of his new creation.